SACRED SOL HEALING INSTITUTE®

Comprehensive Personal Social Development

Mental Health Resilience

The Deconstructing Trauma™

Interactive Workbook Curriculum

Focuses on ASAM Dimensions 3-6 and

Co-occurring Conditions.

Physical, Mental, Emotional, and Spiritual Wellness

Welcome!

FROM SACRED SOL HEALING INSTITUTE
RENEE FRYE

The information used in this interactive curriculum comes from our Deconstructing Trauma Guidebook.

We have built it out into an interactive curriculum based on best practices for professionals, clients, and the general public.

See more at: www.sacredsolhealing.com

BONUS: Download our full-size, color pdf, "Deconstructing Trauma Toolkit," at https://deconstructing-trauma.com/. This is a complimentary gift for you.

Our Toolkit combines all the tools that have been offered throughout the Deconstructing Trauma Guidebook in one convenient reference space, plus bonus material.

Comprehensive Personal Social Development
Deconstructing Trauma™ Interactive Workbook Curriculum

Copyright © 2024. Renee Frye.

ISBN: 979-8-9896548-7-1

Book Production by Transcendent Publishing

Printed in the United States of America.

Walk in Beauty

One of our biggest teachings is learning to "Walk in Beauty" daily, in the world around us as well as in the world inside of us. It requires moral, spiritual, physical, mental, and emotional endurance, integrity, commitment, and patience. "Walking in Beauty" is an intentional life journey; it is a way of life that takes work and dedication. It is not easy, but it is simple.

Many times, life complications will unwind on their own when we are not feeding them with an exhausted, frantic negative mindset. We do not have to become stressed or exhausted to fix what is not working.

The Deconstructing Trauma program teaches us how to "Walk in Beauty," utilizing social development life skills and tools that allow us to step back from the challenges and not take them personally. We do not ignore the challenges, but rather choose a mindset of peace and openness, appreciating the lessons and moving through them, rather than feeding the negativity around them.

These lessons are how we grow in mind, body, and spirit. We have been given the gift of knowledge; if we are able to process, learn, and use this knowledge, it will manifest as wisdom that we can use in our lives. This is how we learn to "Walk in Beauty".

"Walking in Beauty" is challenging, but it is how we live our best life. "Walking in Beauty" doesn't mean that everything is perfect. It means we get to choose how we show up in the world. How we live our best lives, reflecting beauty, grace, strength, light, compassion, resilience, peace, respect, kindness, balance, joy, and love, daily for ourselves and others.

"Walking in Beauty" is the human challenge; it reminds us and teaches us how to respect the sacred hoop of life and all that resides within it. The earth, the elements, the people, and the animals. How can you apply "Walking in Beauty" to your daily life? It is a continual dance filled with highs and lows. You are the medicine; you are the beauty; allow your heart to guide you on this journey to self. You are the miracle you've been looking for, "Walk in Beauty."

2023 - Renee Frye

WELCOME!

Hello, my name is Renee Frye. I am a Trauma-Healing Holistic Specialist and the owner and founder of Sacred Sol Healing Institute® and the Deconstructing Trauma™ Program.

Sacred Sol Healing Institute is more than just an organization; we are a national and global trauma healing movement, a journey to a healthier, happier self. Our healing-centered approach meets each person where they are, offering hope, education, and life wellness support.

Our equitable, evidence-based Deconstructing Trauma Program is available to professionals and the general public through our Deconstructing Trauma guidebook and interactive workbooks, as well as through all of our services and programs.

DECONSTRUCTING TRAUMA | IN SUBSTANCE ABUSE RECOVERY

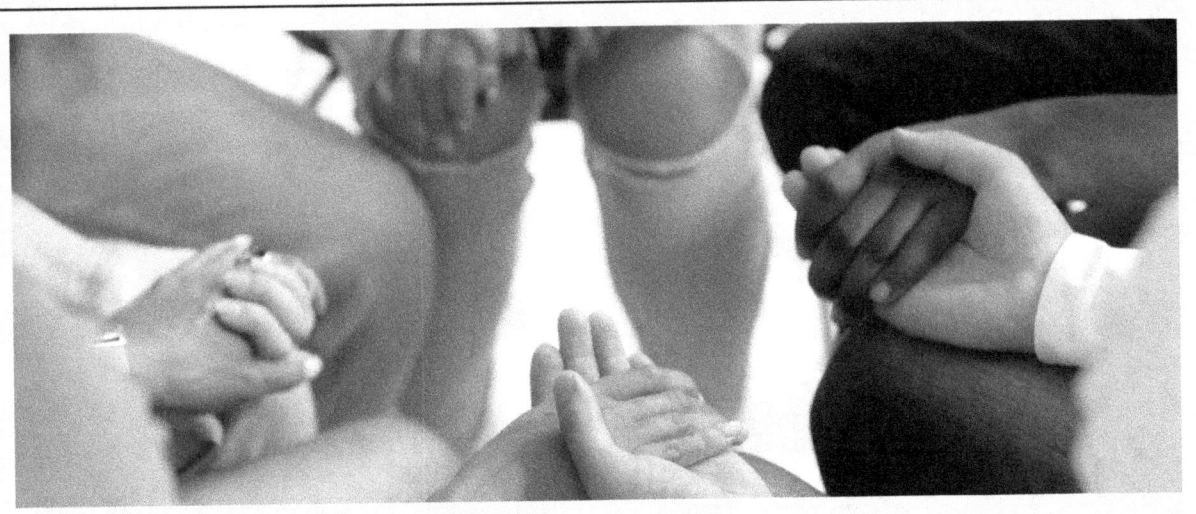

OVERVIEW

DECONSTRUCTING TRAUMA
IN PERSONAL SOCIAL DEVELOPMENT

- The Deconstructing Trauma program teaches a healing-centered life approach, allowing us to safely peel back the layers of trauma that have occurred throughout our lives. By deconstructing our past trauma, we can learn to safely navigate our mental, emotional, physical, and spiritual well-being.

- Our curriculum is based on positive social development; through this process, healthy behaviors, perspectives, and attitudes are learned, offering long-term positive changes in relationships and interactions involving oneself, peers, and family. As we learn to release negative and unhealthy behaviors that have manifested from our trauma, we are able to reprogram to positive mindsets and healthy behaviors. Our program has a significant impact on the release of trauma, chaos, pain, and negativity.

- Through the use of the Deconstructing Trauma Program, individuals can gain a deeper understanding of the root causes of their trauma and work towards healing and growth. The daily awareness tools help individuals become more mindful of their thoughts and behaviors, allowing them to identify triggers and patterns that may be contributing to their trauma. Mindful behavior modification strategies provide practical steps for individuals to shift their patterns and create positive change in their lives.

- The positive behavior resilience method is an approach that focuses on building resilience and strength in the face of adversity. This method helps individuals to reframe negative experiences and emotions, empowering them to find meaning and purpose in their lives. Additionally, energy healing therapy supports the release of stored trauma in the body, allowing individuals to experience a sense of lightness and freedom.

- Overall, the Deconstructing Trauma Program offers a comprehensive and holistic approach to healing trauma. By combining multiple strategies, individuals can experience deep and meaningful transformation, leading to a fulfilling and joyful life.

MODULES

00 | INTRODUCTION

01 | UNDERSTANDING TRAUMA

02 | TRAUMA AND NEGATIVITY

03| DAILY TRIGGERS—LEARNED BEHAVIOR

04 | POSITIVE ACTIONS AND RECOVERY

05 | HEALTHY RELATIONSHIPS

06 | HABITS AND POSITIVE PHRASING

07 | DAILY RESILIENCE AND BALANCE

8| COLLECTIVE TRAUMA HEALING
CONCLUSION

00 DECONSTRUCTING TRAUMA INTRODUCTION
5-28

- 0.1. Unhealthy Continual Crises
- 0.2. Perspective Shifts
- 0.3. Releasing the Struggle Within

01 UNDERSTANDING TRAUMA
29-54

- 1.1. Awareness of Trauma
- 1.2. The Impact of Trauma
- 1.3. Trauma-Informed and Responsive Support

02 TRAUMA AND NEGATIVITY
55-80

- 2.1. Negativity and Trauma
- 2.2. Addiction to Negative Thought Patterns
- 2.3. Mindfulness and Trauma Healing

03 DAILY TRIGGERS—LEARNED BEHAVIOR
81-107

- 3.1. How Trauma Triggers Lead to Unhealthy Patterns
- 3.2. How Negative Dialogues Feed the Trauma Cycle
- 3.3. Trauma Cycles Create Automatic Trauma Responses

04 REPROGRAM TO POSITIVE ACTIONS
108-132

- 4.1. Personal Challenges in Trauma Healing
- 4.2. Labeling and Trauma Projections
- 4.3. Deconstructing Past Trauma

05 HEALTHY RELATIONSHIPS

133-159

- 5.1. Appropriate, Safe, and Healthy Relationships
- 5.2. Healthy Boundaries Keep Us Safe
- 5.3. Non-judgmental Communication

06 HABITS AND POSITIVE PHRASING

160-188

- 6.1. Impacts of Habits in Our Lives
- 6.2. The Power of Positive Rephrasing
- 6.3. Mindful Behavior Modification

07 DAILY HEALING-RESILIENCE AND BALANCE

189-223

- 7.1. Building Resilience and Emotional Strength
- 7.2. Daily Tools Create Healing, Balance, and Resilience
- 7.3. Healing Progress and Wellness Plans

08 CONCLUSION: DECONSTRUCTING TRAUMA

224-240

- 8.1. Committing to Continued Self-Growth
- 8.2. Healing and Processing Trauma
- 8.3. Trauma-Responsive Life Wellness Approach

- **RESOURCE PAGE** 241

0. DECONSTRUCTING TRAUMA INTRODUCTION

<u>Awareness Tool</u>
Moving past our negativities and fears and learning to love ourselves fully and completely is attainable. As we learn how to love ourselves, we can then show the world how we need to be loved.

DECONSTRUCTING TRAUMA INTRODUCTION

MODULE 0

We all have negative tendencies. We are here to learn. This information is only here to raise awareness. It is not an attack on anyone's character.

I used to be the most angry and hateful person I knew. I didn't even realize it; it was a way of life because I felt bad inside. Through years of intensive study and research, I learned that it was okay to look at the challenging toxic behavior patterns I had acquired over time. The day I realized that my behaviors, thoughts, and emotions don't define me was the day that changed my life.

Whhewww! What a relief! I am, of course, responsible for my own actions and behaviors, but knowing that they are not my identity has allowed me to dig deeper into self. What I found was okay; I could change what wasn't appropriate and keep what was! Knowledge gives us the opportunity to evolve and grow.

Even if parts of this book bring up a bit of uncomfortable information, it can be worth your time and effort. Deconstructing Trauma by releasing chaos, pain, and negativity allows healing. It is life-changing!

We live in a very negative, toxic world. Our thoughts are negative, our surroundings are negative; we are led by chaos, pain, and negativity. This is what we know. We are told to suck it up, move on, don't cry, don't show emotions or feelings. We are told that everything is fine... until one day, it's not. No wonder we have extreme behaviors, dependencies, unhappiness, anxiousness, stress, tension, depressive states, anger, addiction, and more.

We haven't been taught to create balance between the body, mind, and spirit. We run blindly from one thing to the next, trying to fulfill our need for support and love by overextending ourselves, which creates continual mental, physical, and spiritual health crises. We unknowingly reach out to find our value and worth in acts of service to others, without realizing that this can be inappropriate and unhealthy if we are using these acts as a catalyst to feel better about ourselves.

Once we realize this, we are able to see that when we are balanced and healthy our value and worth is found within. That of course doesn't mean we need to stop the acts of service and kindness, but maybe we are able to evaluate first why we are doing them. If we are the one who needs to save the world and everyone in it, we will be out of balance. It is dangerous for us, as well as for the people we are "saving."

We each have a responsibility to work through our own experiences so we can resolve trauma, chaos, pain, and suffering. When we rush in to fix it for others, that doesn't allow them to learn or solve their own challenges. They become dependent on us solving their challenges, and we become dependent on solving them so we can feel good about ourselves. This perpetuates the cycle of trauma for both parties.

If we don't tend to our past trauma, we don't know that we can process it and heal.

We have been caught up in an extremely dysfunctional generational "follow-the-leader," not knowing that we can heal, not understanding that we do not have to continue to be a perpetual product of our trauma and suffering. We check-out with drugs, alcohol, food, social media, gambling, shopping, anger, passive-aggressive behavior, controlling others, withdrawing, and more. Negativity affects us in every way. It is poisonous to the body, mind, and spirit. It manifests as disease — physically, mentally, emotionally, and spiritually.

The more familiar we are with something, the easier it is to get back to it. We have become so familiar with chaos, pain, and negativity that it is our new normal. Our bodies have become used to living in fight-or-flight. And because the body is not meant to continually live in fight-or-flight, it begins to break down. From there, we become frantic. We become sick, and then eventually we need to be sick; we are labeled with a diagnosis and we feel validated in our discomfort.

What if we shifted that thought process for a moment? What if we started to consider the option of healing, of not becoming our diagnosis? What if we were open to the possibility that we could process and release trauma, misery, and suffering, and, along with that, reduce the dis-ease of the body, mind, and spirit? Of course, there are times a diagnosis is valid, and medication is necessary. But so much of what's going on in our world can be improved if we are open to the possibility of change and committing to the steps that bring about that change.

Bringing in awareness, knowledge, and action can change our lives. When we are aware of our actions, our thoughts and our emotions, we are able to understand, process, and commit to the action of releasing our negative experiences. In this way, we learn that we are not our experiences; they are not who we are.

Instead, the experience manifests as a learning opportunity. We can learn and release the challenges and lessons because they are no longer needed, instead of holding onto them, pushing them down where they grow and become toxic, poisoning us and negatively affecting our daily lives.

Toxic stress and negativity have the power to damage all portions of our lives. Learning to identify our addiction to chaos, pain, and negativity is crucial. Not only is it okay to see and understand this predicament, but it is appropriate to learn how and why we are addicted to negativity.

By learning and arming ourselves with knowledge and tools, we can mitigate (lessen), and release toxic stress and negativity. We can live in freedom, peace, love, happiness, safety, and joy! Through this journey to self, we learn to understand our daily triggers and learned behavior. What we find along the way is okay because we are not our trauma, we are not our pain, we are not our suffering, we are not our feelings, we are not our emotions, we are not our experiences.

These things come to us so we can learn and evolve, not suffer and punish ourselves. When we release negativity, we are able to heal trauma. As we seek change, we are able to reprogram to positive behaviors, thoughts, and actions.

Whatever we are most familiar with, we come back to easier. So, as we begin to shift the familiarity of negativity, we begin to release and resolve toxic stress, triggers, and negative learned behavior patterns that have caused pain and suffering in our lives.

Suffering is imminent in general, especially when there is no hope or change. At times, circumstances or events may feel like they are happening to us for no other reason than to hurt us. We may identify ourselves in that pain and damage, which then increases our suffering. Suffering is part of how we learn and heal. When we are willing to look at the discomfort that has caused the suffering, we are able to begin healing.

Through shadow work—seeing, observing, resolving, and releasing our dark and negative tendencies, impulses, and experiences—we are better able to understand our challenges and move past the pain and suffering.

As we begin to realize that we can shift and release the feelings and experiences that cause suffering, we learn that suffering can be changed.

This comes about by allowing a new perspective: "It's not happening to me, it's just happening." *Note: We are not referring to victim crimes. If you have been the victim of a crime, please reach out to trusted support, such as a family member or friend, contact law enforcement, and seek out appropriate medical and mental health care professionals.

By understanding and resolving suffering, we are able to differentiate between suffering and struggling. Struggling is much different from suffering. Struggling is uncomfortable, whereas suffering is an unbearable, unchanging state of despair and hopelessness. Both are necessary to learn and evolve, but suffering does not have to be a constant part of our lives.

Once we resolve the chaos, pain, negativity, anger, fear, guilt, shame, grief, abandonment, self-loathing, and toxicity that have entered our lives, we are able to release suffering and change our lives in a positive way. As we learn to understand, let go, and heal suffering, we can see that general life struggles are also inevitable and necessary; we must struggle to grow.

Struggling is part of the process; only through the struggle can we gain the strength we need to move forward to the next space. As things fall apart they will rebuild in the intended way. It is part of rebirth and transformation.

Through this insight we understand it is okay to not be okay; it is okay to be uncomfortable and struggle; it is temporary and has purpose. The butterfly must struggle to break out of the cocoon because it needs to build the strength in its wings to fly. If we open the cocoon so the butterfly doesn't have to struggle, it will die because it hasn't had the opportunity to create strength in its wings.

We can apply this knowledge to our daily lives, realizing that struggling is part of creating strength and learning balance. Through this wisdom, we begin to look forward to coming out on the other side, stronger and wiser, knowing that the lesson will pass instead of suffering, feeling doomed, and being subject to our misery, which would have created more suffering.

We are able to achieve lasting change in our lives as we reprogram to positivity. Through this process, with the appropriate tools and information, we begin to develop healthy relationships, not only with the world around us but especially with ourselves and the world inside of us.

Understanding how to speak in positive, trauma-sensitive language changes our lives and the lives around us. We gain empowerment, resilience, and balance through learning techniques and positive options to incorporate into our daily lives.

We are not meant to be miserable; we are meant to thrive in positivity, love, and joy. No one else can do this for us, only we can be the change we seek. Each one of us has infinite worth and value. Our value and our worth is not defined by our actions; however, our actions may not always reflect our value and worth. The key is to learn from our experiences and move forward, evolving and growing.

No matter where you've been, no matter what you've done, no matter what has happened to you, your worth, your value, is infinite. It always has been and always will be. Here, we peel back the layers to access that space. Everything you need is contained within.

Through this information, and by utilizing these tools, you can release chaos, pain, and negativity. You can discover the missing peace. We all struggle, we can all heal. You are not alone. You are the miracle you've been looking for.

Welcome to the Deconstructing Trauma Program.

WORKSHEET 1

◆ What did you learn about Trauma from the Introduction?

◆ What insight did you gain about others and their Trauma from the Introduction?

◆ What information in the Introduction can assist you in understanding Trauma in your life?

◆ What part of the Introduction empowered you?

WORKSHEET 2

Often trauma can lead to substance abuse. Many of us have been affected by substance abuse in our own lives or in the lives of friends and family.

Substance abuse definitions.

- Definition. The habit of taking too much of a harmful drug or drinking too much alcohol. https://www.oxfordlearnersdictionaries.com/us/definition/english/substance-abuse

- Definition. As used in this discussion, substance abuse refers to excessive use of a drug in a way that is detrimental to self, society, or both. This definition includes both physical dependence and psychologic dependence. https://www.ncbi.nlm.nih.gov/books/NBK319/#:~:text=Definition,physical%20dependence%20and%20psychologic%20dependence.

- Definition. A drug is any substance that changes the way you think, feel, or behave. https://myhealth.alberta.ca/Alberta/Pages/Substance-use-common-drugs.aspx

Commonly Used Drugs

- Alcohol, Ayahuasca, Cannabis (Marijuana/Pot/Weed)
- Central Nervous System Depressants (Benzos), Cocaine (Coke/Crack)
- Fentanyl, GHB, Hallucinogens, Heroin, Inhalants, Ketamine, Khat, Kratom
- LSD (Acid), MDMA (Ecstasy/Molly), Mescaline (Peyote)
- Methamphetamine (Crystal/Meth), PCP (Angel Dust)
- Over-the-Counter-Loperamide and Dextromethorphan (DXM)
- Prescription Opioids (Oxy/Percs), Prescription Stimulants (Speed)
- Psilocybin (Magic Mushrooms/Shrooms), Rohypnol® (Flunitrazepam/Roofies)
- Salvia, Steroids (Anabolic), Synthetic Cannabinoids (K2/Spice)
- Synthetic Cathinones (Bath Salts/Flakka), Tobacco/Nicotine and Vaping.

https://nida.nih.gov/research-topics/commonly-used-drugs-charts

What is your personal definition of substance abuse? How have you been affected by trauma-related substance abuse ?

DIMENSIONS OF WELLNESS

Each choice we make in our lives results in positive or negative consequences. Observe how an unhealthy continual crises can stem from trauma cycles and how this affects all areas of our lives.

ENVIRONMENTAL

INTELLECTUAL

PHYSICAL

OCCUPATIONAL

SPIRITUAL

SOCIAL

FINANCIAL

EMOTIONAL

SUBSTANCE ABUSE

Continue on to the next page to read and explore the eight dimensions of wellness by SAMHSA.

• UNHEALTHY CONTINUAL CRISES

How Do the Eight Dimensions of Wellness Affect Your Life?

Wellness is a term we all know and use often, but what exactly is it, and what does it mean for a person to be well? According to the Substance Abuse and Mental Health Services Administration (SAMSHA), wellness means overall well-being. It incorporates the mental, emotional, physical, occupational, intellectual, and spiritual aspects of a person's life. Each aspect of wellness can affect the overall quality of life, so it's important to consider all aspects of health. This is especially important for people with mental health and substance use conditions because wellness directly relates to the quality and longevity of your life (1).

The eight dimensions of wellness are emotional, environmental, financial, intellectual, occupational, physical, social, and spiritual. All are very important to someone's overall well-being. In the coming paragraphs, I will explain, in more detail, each dimension and also give you a few ways to make improvements in each dimension.

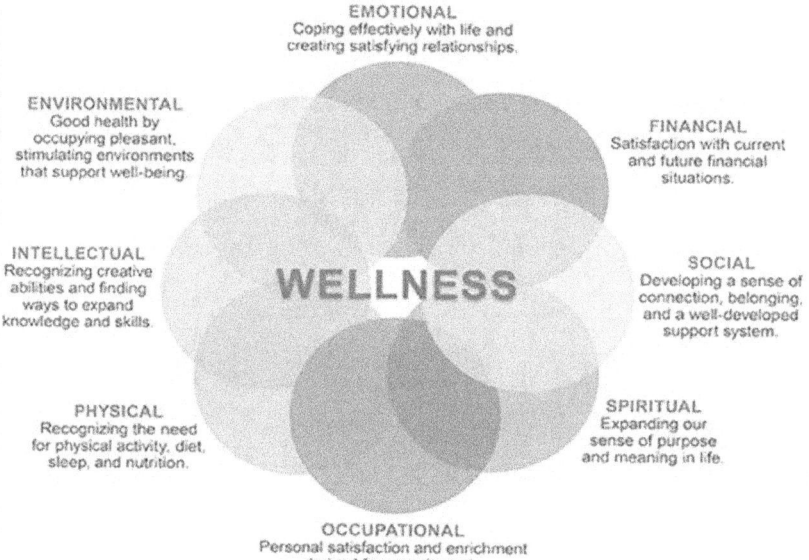

Emotional wellness is the ability to cope effectively with life and create satisfying relationships. Life has a way of throwing us curve balls, which can be very difficult at times. The relationships we create and nurture give us a shoulder to lean on when that curve ball comes our way. One way to improve emotional wellness is to put a positive spin on life situations. Try to cultivate a positive feeling even during negative times throughout your life. This is much easier said than done, but with practice, it can be achieved. You do need to be mentally aware of your emotions, and when a negative feeling arises, attempt to change it into a positive one. Playing a favorite song, chatting with a close friend, or playing with a pet are just a few examples of how to cultivate positive feelings.

Rejection and loss are two major issues that can have a big impact on our emotional well-being. It's important to recognize the feelings you have during times of rejection and loss, but it is also important not to dwell on them or remain in that negative emotional state. Remind yourself how much worth you have by listing the positive attributes you possess in the area of life in which you were rejected, whether it's your work life, dating life, social life, etc. Finding meaning in a loss can be difficult, but it can improve your emotional well-being.

You may want to develop a greater appreciation for those who are still here, reevaluate your values and ideals, or honor what or who has been lost. These are only a few examples of how to find meaning during a time of loss. Emotional wellness doesn't mean avoiding bad or difficult times; rather, it's the ability to cope effectively during them.

Environmental wellness means good health by occupying pleasant, stimulating environments that support well-being. It's important to feel good about where you live, work, play, and wherever else you may spend time. Good health for the planet is also a major part of environmental wellness. Here are a few ways to improve your environmental well-being.

The first is an obvious one. Clean and organize your living space. Then clean and organize your workspace. After these two tasks are done, you should feel a greater sense of comfort and much less anxiety. This is a big boost for your environmental well-being. Now it's time to take a look at the big picture, and that's the planet we live on. Start recycling, use less water, and pick up trash when you come across it on the ground. We have to live in this environment, so it's important that each of us do our part to keep it clean.

Financial Wellness is the satisfaction of your current and future financial situations. It's not about how much you make that makes you financially well, but rather, are you satisfied with how much you make? Someone who makes $30,000 a year could be more financially well than someone who makes $100,000 per year. It's a proven fact that those who are financially well are more productive at work. Planning is the key to attaining financial wellness. It's important to plan a budget, set goals, plan a saving strategy, and plan for retirement. These are just a few of the plans that need to be made to have financial wellness in your life. Once the planning is complete, it's time to stick to your plans and put them into action. A savings plan will create financial margins in your life for those unexpected car/house repairs or whatever else might come up that will cost you money. Taking these steps will help guide you to a financially well future.

Intellectual Wellness means recognizing creative abilities and finding ways to expand knowledge and skills. A person who is intellectually well never stops learning. They're thirsty for knowledge and recognize that there is so much more to be learned. There is a certain feeling you get when you achieve something that you have never done before. It's that positive feeling that drives us to become more intellectually well. Some ways to improve your intellectual wellness are to improve time management, remove objectivity, and improve your critical thinking. It's important to make time for reading a book or learning a new hobby. Remove objectivity by keeping an open mind about new ideas, insights, thoughts, expressions, and values. Always question and keep your brain active, and you will begin to improve your intellectual wellness.

Occupational Wellness is the personal satisfaction and enrichment of one's work. You need to feel a sense of contribution and achievement in the work that you do. Developing occupational wellness allows you to communicate your values through whatever work you choose to do. This could be paid work or unpaid work. Here are some ideas on how you can improve your occupational wellness. Start by reflecting on what occupations will leave you feeling gratified. Look into the tasks you enjoy doing. Also, think about what occupational tasks you dislike and find burdensome. Search for volunteer work that you find interesting. Also, set career goals for yourself and constantly work toward achieving those goals. Taking these steps will lead you to have more occupational wellness in your life.

Physical Wellness means recognizing the need for physical activity. Exercise offers many benefits for a person's overall well-being. It improves your chances of living longer and healthier, relieves symptoms of depression and anxiety, improves your mood, and prevents weight gain. Exercise is just one facet of being physically well. Taking care of your physical body by showering, brushing your teeth, and going to the doctor for checkups are all ways to improve your physical wellness. Treating the body with respect will ultimately lead you to be more physically well.

Social Wellness is developing a sense of connection, belonging, and a well-developed support system. This is why spending quality time with close friends is so important. One of the best things you could do to become more socially well is to become a contributing member of your community. You can volunteer, and at the same time, you will meet new people and gain new social skills. Communication is a key factor in becoming socially well. Good communication skills will allow you to resolve problems that you may have with other people that you socialize with on a day-to-day basis. These are a few ideas to help you become more socially well.

Spiritual wellness means expanding our sense of purpose and meaning in life. Spiritual wellness is unique to everyone. It's the deepest part of you that gives meaning to your life. Some ways to improve spiritual wellness are to meditate, pray, and listen to affirmations. A spiritually well person is okay with spending time alone and reflecting. It's important to take time to search for the things that provide meaning in your life. It could be your beliefs, values, and morals that give meaning to your life. Make sure that these things guide the decisions you make as you live out your life. Practice these tips, and you will become more spiritually well.

These eight dimensions of wellness all play an important role in our lives. Focus on the areas that you are weak in and start from there; it can seem a bit overwhelming if you try to change everything at once. As you work in the areas where you're struggling the most, you will find that stress in your life will start to decrease and positive feelings will start to increase. You'll begin to produce more feel-good neurotransmitters like dopamine and serotonin. Life will surely be more enjoyable.

WORKSHEET 3

List a few words that describe the negative consequences that have developed in each dimension of your life from traumatic experiences.

Example

| 1 | Emotional | 1 | Pain, sad, angry, lonely, hopeless. |

THE EIGHT DIMENSIONS OF WELLNESS		NEGATIVE CONSEQUENCES OF UNRESOLVED TRAUMA	
1	EMOTIONAL	1	
2	FINANCIAL	2	
3	SOCIAL	3	
4	SPIRITUAL	4	
5	OCCUPATIONAL	5	
6	PHYSICAL	6	
7	INTELLECTUAL	7	
8	ENVIRONMENTAL	8	

Examine how you can shift your thoughts and perspectives to develop healthy pattern in each dimension of your life as you move forward in your wellness journey.

WORKSHEET 4

List a few words that describe the positive consequences or rewards that can develop in each dimension of your life from shifting to a positive perspective in your wellness journey.

Example

1	Emotional	1	Happy inside, peaceful, self-worth, valuable.

	THE EIGHT DIMENSIONS OF WELLNESS		POSITIVE CONSEQUENCES OF MY WELLNESS JOURNEY
1	EMOTIONAL	1	
2	FINANCIAL	2	
3	SOCIAL	3	
4	SPIRITUAL	4	
5	OCCUPATIONAL	5	
6	PHYSICAL	6	
7	INTELLECTUAL	7	
8	ENVIRONMENTAL	8	

Consider healthy strategies and goals to bring positive consequences into your life.

WORKSHEET 5

List healthy strategies and goals to bring positive
consequences into your life.

TOP 3 PRIORITIES TO BRING POSITIVE CONSEQUENCES INTO YOUR LIFE

1

2

3

BRAINSTORM HEALTHY STRATEGIES AND GOALS TO BRING POSITIVE CONSEQUENCES INTO YOUR LIFE

• PERSPECTIVE SHIFTS

WORKSHEET 6

Releasing the Struggle Within. Answer the
questions below.

"The Struggle Within"

◆ What unhealthy coping mechanisms have you developed?

◆ What do you struggle with before you use an unhealthy coping method?

◆ What do you struggle with during an unhealthy coping episode?

◆ What do you struggle with after an unhealthy coping episode?

◆ What are healthier ways to release those struggles?

Read "Embodying Grace" on the next page.

Embodying Grace

Grace is what emerges from the struggle... Grace is the courage to face the uncomfortable

Grace is our true raw self exposed. Not only in spite of but because of our flaws, this is how we learn. Grace allows us to take our struggles, our trials, our lessons and turn them into wisdom.

Through this Grace, we know we are not our trauma, we are not our suffering, we learn our lessons and move on. Grace allows us to separate negative feelings, triggers, and experiences from our identity.

Grace knows the struggle is real but allows us to release the struggle. We are not the struggle, we are not the pain, we are not the suffering. We are not alone.

Grace is humility in action; humility is not shame.

Being humble takes courage, strength, balance, and Grace.

Grace allows us to support and love others without controlling, manipulating, or running their lives.

Grace allows us to evolve from our trauma.

Grace allows us to let others walk their own journey, without rushing in fixing, saving, and taking away their opportunity for lessons and growth.

Grace allows us to trust others to handle their own journey, not in the way we see fit but in the way that is best served for them. They will learn their lesson... or they won't; this is not up to us. It is our responsibility to be mindful and care for ourselves by removing ourselves from unhealthy situations. It is not our responsibility to change anyone else or make them see the light.

Grace allows us to release this to a higher space, a higher presence. In this way, we learn not to take situations personally.

Grace tells us it's not always about us...What a relief!

Grace allows us to fully and completely love and accept ourselves at the most basic fundamental level.

Grace is our true self realized. Our true self is Love, Light, and Grace.

Grace Embodied...Is You.

Renee Spiritflyer Frye 2022

WORKSHEET 7

Releasing the Struggle Within. After reading "Embodying Grace," answer the questions below.

"Releasing the Struggle Within"

◆ How can Grace help you release the struggle with repeated trauma cycles?

◆ What did you learn from reading Embodying Grace?

◆ How can you apply this in your daily life?

NOTES:

Continue to Module 0 Quiz on the next page.

• RELEASING THE STRUGGLE WITHIN

QUIZ ✶ MODULE 0

TRUE   FALSE

1 We run blindly from one thing to the next, trying to fulfill our need for support and love by overextending ourselves, which creates continual mental, physical, and spiritual health crises.

2 If we don't tend to our past trauma, we can still process it and heal.

3 Negativity affects us in every way. It is poisonous to the body, mind, and spirit. It manifests as disease — physically, mentally, emotionally, and spiritually.

4 Our bodies have become used to living in fight-or-flight. Because the body is not meant to continually live in fight-or-flight, it begins to break down.

5 Being open to the possibility of change and committing to the steps that bring about that change will not improve our lives.

6 When we are aware of our actions, our thoughts and our emotions, we are able to understand, process, and commit to the action of releasing our negative experiences.

7 We are not our experiences; they are not who we are. Our experiences are learning opportunities.

8 Toxic stress and negativity does not damage all portions of our lives.

9 Understanding how to speak in positive, trauma-sensitive language does not change our lives.

10 Our value and our worth is not defined by our actions; however, our actions may not always reflect our value and worth. The key is to learn from our experiences and move forward, evolving and growing.

SELF CHECK-IN — SCALE 0-10

Take an inventory of where you are. There are no rights or wrongs; this is a self-reflective check-in to see where you are doing well or where you want to improve. Rate statements below from 0 to 10.

1   I would like to change trauma cycles in my life.

2   I am happy with my life.

3   I have a good relationship with myself.

4   I have healthy family relationships.

5   I have healthy relationships with partners.

6   I have a legal job that pays my bills.

7   I have healthy coping skills.

8   I am mindful of my nutrition daily.

9   I am in nature every day.

10   I get physical exercise daily.

We all struggle, We can all heal. You are not alone.

MODULE JOURNAL

You are the miracle You've been looking for.

QUIZ ✳ MODULE 0 (ANSWERS)

		TRUE	FALSE
1	We run blindly from one thing to the next, trying to fulfill our need for support and love by overextending ourselves, which creates continual mental, physical, and spiritual health crises.	✓	
2	If we don't tend to our past trauma, we can still process it and heal.		✓
3	Negativity affects us in every way. It is poisonous to the body, mind, and spirit. It manifests as disease — physically, mentally, emotionally, and spiritually.	✓	
4	Our bodies have become used to living in fight-or-flight. Because the body is not meant to continually live in fight-or-flight, it begins to break down.	✓	
5	Being open to the possibility of change and committing to the steps that bring about that change will not improve our lives.		✓
6	When we are aware of our actions, our thoughts and our emotions, we are able to understand, process, and commit to the action of releasing our negative experiences.	✓	
7	We are not our experiences; they are not who we are. Our experiences are learning opportunities.	✓	
8	Toxic stress and negativity does not damage all portions of our lives.		✓
9	Understanding how to speak in positive, trauma-sensitive language does not change our lives.		✓
10	Our value and our worth is not defined by our actions; however, our actions may not always reflect our value and worth. The key is to learn from our experiences and move forward, evolving and growing.	✓	

MODULE 0 SUMMARY

1 ### COURSE TAKEAWAY POINT ONE
- 0.1. Unhealthy Continual Crises. Unhealthy continual crises occur from unresolved trauma and pain, resulting in unhealthy coping mechanisms. This creates a continual trauma cycle that we pass on from generation to generation, until resolved.

2 ### COURSE TAKEAWAY POINT TWO
- 0.2. Perspective Shifts. Perspective shifts can change our perception. When we begin to perceive ourselves as capable and good enough, it will begin to change our lives. Our perception shapes our reality.

3 ### COURSE TAKEAWAY POINT THREE
- 0.3. Releasing the Struggle Within. As we begin to release the struggle within, we begin to understand Grace. Grace allows us to evolve from our trauma, to learn, and to release toxic repeated cycles that bring us pain and suffering. Our trauma is not who we are. We are love, we are light, and we are grace.

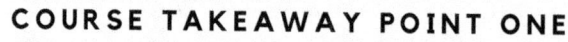

1 ### YOUR TAKEAWAY POINT ONE
- 0.1. Unhealthy Continual Crises.

2 ### YOUR TAKEAWAY POINT TWO
- 0.2. Perspective Shifts.

3 ### YOUR TAKEAWAY POINT THREE
- 0.3. Releasing the Struggle Within.

DECONSTRUCTING TRAUMA
IN PERSONAL SOCIAL DEVELOPMENT

1. UNDERSTANDING
TRAUMA

<u>Awareness Tool</u>
When we begin to give ourselves permission
to feel, along with the appropriate tools to
process our feelings and heal our trauma, it
can change our lives.

UNDERSTANDING TRAUMA

MODULE 1

DT Book Chapter 1: Awareness

The Journey of Deconstructing Trauma Starts with Awareness.

What is Awareness? Why is it Important?
Awareness is understanding what our surroundings are and acknowledging our presence within the space. Awareness is important because when we are aware of the environment around us and inside of us we are able to make different choices and decisions. We have the ability to choose what happens in our lives when we are aware of what is transpiring around us.

What is Self-Awareness? Why is it Important?
Self-awareness is the ability to pay attention to yourself and how your actions, thoughts, and feelings match or don't match your own standards. Self-awareness is important because it allows us to see why we might have an issue, how we are acting, and why we are acting that way. It also allows us to see why others might have an issue, how they are acting, and why they are acting that way.

General awareness and self-awareness can have a huge impact on substance abuse recovery. When we are aware of the environment around us as well as inside of us, we can make healthy, appropriate, and safe choices.

Highly self-aware people are able to interpret their actions, emotions, and thoughts without feeling bad about themselves. It is a unique talent because many of us perceive our circumstances based solely on our emotions, rather than actual facts.

Being self-aware is crucial because it enables us to evaluate our progress and effectiveness and alter our course as needed. Through true self-awareness, we are able to choose the way we interact with ourselves and the world around us. As we learn to understand our reactions, we can then begin to understand our emotions. We resolve our negative experiences rather than ignoring our feelings, perpetuating a toxic cycle.

Many of us have been taught at a young age to ignore, minimize, or repress our emotions. We have to push them down; we are not allowed to have a feeling that someone doesn't want to hear. "Quit crying"; "Don't be a sissy"; "Grow up"; "Don't cry;"; "Don't be mad," et cetera. The only problem with that is we DO have feelings, so when we push them down and pretend that they are not there, they begin to poison us inside. This creates a mix of chaos, pain, and negativity.

We develop toxic trauma as these suppressed emotions poison us, leading to anger, rage, guilt, shame, depressive states, grief, anxiousness, addiction, drugs, alcohol, despair, disease, eating disorders, identity crises, and more.

Self-awareness is a remarkable tool that allows us to gain insight into our own habits and perceptions that may be harmful to our well-being. Self-awareness allows us to see our trauma through a new lens. We are not our trauma, we are not our pain, and we are not our suffering. This is something we have experienced, but it is not who we are; it is not our identity.

What is Trauma? Why it is Important?
Trauma is a profoundly stressful or upsetting event. Trauma can take various forms, including psychological, physical, emotional, sexual, and domestic abuse. We all have trauma because we have all had negative experiences in our lives. These negative experiences are referred to as trauma, and they affect our interactions with the world around us as well as the world inside of us. Trauma is prevalent in our lives and can comprise human potential and diminish life quality. One of the primary causes of disorder, disability, illness, and mortality is trauma.

Trauma is important because it has and will continue to impact our lives in negative ways until we take an active role in healing and resolving it. Through this space we learn to observe, discovering awareness of the situation and the challenge, without becoming the situation or the challenge.

Our daily experiences will continue to negatively affect us until we learn to understand our trauma responses. These trauma responses are meant to keep us alive. We are programmed to protect ourselves, either by submission and backing away or by anger and fighting back. Different situations, as well as different personalities and past experiences, will dictate how we respond in certain situations.

Many times, our past trauma can serve as a learned lesson that can keep us safe, moving forward. For example: We learn the stove is hot by touching it and burning our hand, however, that experience keeps us from continuing to touch it and burn ourselves.

Understanding our learned triggers and impulses is so important; they can teach us how to identify the difference between a real threat or a perceived threat and can change the course of events.

An impulse is a powerful, sudden urge to take action. These impulses can save our lives. Impulses are bound to happen from our environment; we do not have to act like it's okay and everything is fine if we have learned experience that shows us something is dangerous or not healthy.

A trigger will lead to the impulse; when that happens we can stop and make a choice. We don't have to make choices based on reactions and impulses.

Trauma is important because it has and will continue to impact our lives in negative ways until it is resolved. Unresolved trauma leads to many addictions, manifesting in unhealthy patterns of drug and alcohol abuse, eating disorders, excessive gambling, self-harm, and suicide.

Our past trauma does and will continue to affect our lives until we take an active role in healing that trauma. The first step is understanding our trauma.

The Aces (Adverse Childhood Experiences) Study provides insight on the effects that trauma has had on us as we grew up.

What are Adverse Childhood Experiences (ACEs)? Why are they Important?

Adverse childhood experiences, or ACEs, are potentially stressful events that may occur during childhood are known as adverse childhood experiences (0-17 years). ACEs are linked to long-term health problems, mental illness, and problems with using drugs or alcohol as a teen or adult. ACEs are important because they can damage a person's ability to learn, get a job, and make money; however, preventing ACEs is possible. The ACEs Study can help us identify trauma that has occurred in our lives. Once we are aware of our trauma we can take steps to release and heal this trauma.

We are not placing blame or passing off our current actions because we are identifying our past trauma. Through this experience we are learning more about our challenges so we can identify, resolve, and evolve!

We live in a re-traumatized state to some extent until we are able to release our trauma and start reprogramming negative learned behavior.

What is Re-traumatization? Why is it Important?

A re-traumatization is an intentional or unintentional reminder of past trauma that triggers a reoccurrence of the original traumatic event. A circumstance, an attitude or expression, or specific situations that mimic the dynamics (loss of power, control, or safety) of the initial trauma might trigger it. Triggering re-traumatization is important because when we are unaware we can inadvertently re-traumatize and continue this dangerous cycle in our lives, causing chaos, harm, and addiction.

Some of the main causes of re-traumatization are: Feeling like you don't have control, going through changes you didn't expect, feeling threatened or attacked, feeling weak, discouraged, low, scared, or feeling shame.

So where does this leave us??? Are we doomed to live in our trauma forever??? Absolutely Not!!!!

We do have free will and can exercise that free will! We can choose to address and release our past trauma and learn how to reprogram ourselves to a positive mindset, thus changing the course of our unhealthy patterns.

We can begin this healing journey by seeking Trauma-Informed and Trauma-Responsive services and resources.

What is Trauma-Informed Approach? Why is it Important?
A Trauma-Informed approach means speaking to the person about the trauma that happened without calling them "bad" or "broken." A Trauma-Informed approach means that you understand, plan for, and respond to each person's experience, hopes, and special needs.

A Trauma-Informed approach starts with knowing how trauma affects a person on a physical, social, mental, and emotional level.

There are three parts to a Trauma-Informed approach.
1. Being aware of how prevalent trauma is.
2. Being aware of how trauma affects everyone.
3. Acting on this knowledge by putting it to use.

Each person's experience of trauma can be different, which can test their coping skills and cause them to start utilizing survival strategies.

Trauma may be the result of a single event (for instance, a natural disaster or seeing or being a victim of violence) or a series of events (long-term abuse). Trauma changes how we see ourselves ("I'm helpless"; "I'm worth[l]less"); how we see the world ("The world is dangerous, no one can protect me"); and how we see our relationships with other people ("I cannot trust anyone.") These ideas affect how we act toward ourselves and the rest of the world.

A Trauma-Informed approach is important because with this approach we avoid re-traumatizing or blaming individuals for trying to manage their traumatic reactions. Understanding the physical, social, and emotional consequences of trauma is the first step in a Trauma-Informed approach, this allows the individual to be met where they are at and to heal and overcome their trauma.

The Key Concepts: Trauma-Informed Care are: Safety, Trustworthiness, Choice, Collaboration, Empowerment.

What are the Benefits of Trauma-Informed Care?
The benefits of Trauma-Informed care are that we are able to realize our past trauma, identify how the trauma has affected us, and respond with positive decisive action to release and reprogram this trauma.

This process changes negative learned behavior, reprograms unhealthy thought patterns, and redirects our lives in a good way.

Putting our newfound knowledge into practice allows us to receive the desired outcome of positive change in our lives.

And finally, we reach Trauma-Responsive Care. Trauma-Informed is where it starts, and Trauma-Responsive takes it to the next level and puts the Trauma-Informed theory into action, allowing healing!

What is Trauma-Responsive Care? Why is it Important?
Trauma-Responsive care is attempting to resolve problems in a helpful and understanding way. Trauma-Sensitive approaches ask, "What's happening?" or "How can I help?" rather than, "What's the matter with you?"

Trauma-Responsive care is important because it has a significant favorable effect on future levels of addiction, criminality, violence, and other societal disorders. Trauma-Responsive care is crucial. It provides compassion, hope, and encouragement. It offers sympathy, support, and hope. How can we assist and heal? It provides strategies, solutions, life-changing information, plans of action, and resources for minimizing and resolving past trauma.

What are the Benefits of Trauma-Responsive Care?
The benefits of Trauma-Responsive care are lasting change and improved whole health and wellness. By applying and implementing the Deconstructing Trauma principles and tools, we are able to reprogram and release trauma triggers and negative learned behavior.

With our newfound awareness, we can begin to seek modalities that allow us to heal and assist us in positive, productive ways. We can all participate in Trauma-Responsive care toward ourselves and others. This brings us hope and improves relationships with ourselves and others.

WORKSHEET 1

◆ What did you learn about awareness from this module?

◆ What insight did you obtain about others and awareness of their Trauma from this module?

◆ What information in this module can assist you in understanding Trauma in your own life?

◆ What part of this module empowered you?

WORKSHEET 2

Awareness Tools in Understanding Trauma.

- *Awareness Tool: We are not responsible for other people's actions, but we are responsible for changing our actions, releasing trauma, and healing from the past.*

- *Awareness Tool: Trauma is part of all of our stories, but it's not who we are. Life is full of learning experiences that are meant to challenge us to grow and evolve. We can choose to reduce our suffering, but it will take effort and action to manifest. By choosing to do nothing we are also making a choice.*

Awareness of the negative effects of unresolved trauma.

- What is your personal definition of trauma?

- How has trauma affected your life?

If you are able to, list your physical, mental/emotional, and spiritual trauma.

Continue on to the ACEs study.

What is the ACEs Study and Why is it Important?

Potentially traumatic events that may occur during childhood (0-17 years) are known as adverse childhood experiences (ACEs).

Description of Adverse childhood experiences (ACEs).. Adverse childhood experiences (ACEs) can have a significant impact on the outcome of an individual's life. Potentially stressful events that may occur during childhood (0-17 years) are known as adverse childhood experiences (ACEs).

ACEs can have long-term detrimental repercussions on health, well-being, and life chances such as education and employment. These factors may increase the risk of injury, sexually transmitted infections, personal physical and mental health challenges, teen pregnancy, pregnancy issues, fetal death, sex trafficking, cancer, diabetes, heart disease, or suicide.

For example, being hurt by violence, abuse, or neglect, seeing violence at home or in the community, or having a family member try or die by suicide are all examples of traumatic events. There are also things in the child's environment that can make them feel less safe, stable, and connected; for example, if you grew up in a home where there were problems with drugs or mental health, where there was a lot of chaos because your parents split up, or where someone in the home went to jail/prison. These are not the only negative outcomes that can occur. There are a lot of other traumatic events that could potentially harm physical, mental, emotional, and spiritual health and happiness.

ACEs are linked to long-term health problems, mental illness, and problems with using drugs or alcohol as a teen or adult. ACEs can also damage a person's ability to learn, get a job, and make money; however, preventing ACEs is possible.

Awareness Tool: ACEs are relevant because they may have long-lasting, negative impacts on health, happiness, and may reduce options for education and employment. RF

ACEs and other social factors that affect health, like living in poor or racially segregated neighborhoods, moving a lot, or not having enough food, can cause toxic stress (extended or prolonged stress). Toxic stress from ACEs can hurt a child's brain development, immune system, and ability to deal with stress. Changes like these can affect a child's ability to pay attention, make decisions, and learn.

When children are young, toxic stress can make it hard for them to make healthy, stable relationships. They may also have unstable jobs as adults and have problems with money, jobs, and depressive states throughout their lives. Consequently, these issues may be passed on to future generations. Some children may be exposed to more toxic stress because of past and ongoing traumas caused by racism, or the effects of poverty caused by a lack of educational and job opportunities. i

Awareness Tool: The ACEs Study: Adverse Childhood Experiences. It is important because this study can help us identify trauma that has occurred in our lives. RF

Below is the Aces Study Questioner, a quick survey that can help identify trauma that has occurred in our lives. This is referred to as "lived trauma." The information below comes from multiple listed sources. Knowing how and why our past trauma has affected us offers unique healing opportunities and insight and increases general trauma awareness, as well as self- awareness.

Adverse Childhood Experience (ACE) Questionnaire ii

This asks questions about events that happened during your childhood; specifically, the first 18 years of your life. The information you provide by answering these yes or no questions will allow us to better understand problems that may have occurred early in life and how those problems may be impacting the challenges you are experiencing today. Write YES or NO for each question. Each "yes" response will equal one point.

While you were growing up, during your first 18 years of life:

1. Did a parent or other adult in the household often:

Swear at you, insult you, put you down, or humiliate you? OR Act in a way that made you afraid that you might be physically hurt?

Yes or No... If Yes, enter 1 _____

2. Did a parent or other adult in the household often:

Push, grab, slap, or throw something at you? OR Ever hit you so hard that you had marks or were injured?

Yes or No... If Yes, enter 1 _____

3. Did an adult or person at least 5 years older than you ever:

Touch or fondle you or have you touch their body in a sexual way? OR Attempt or actually have oral, anal, or vaginal intercourse with you?

Yes or No... If Yes, enter 1 _____

4. Did you often feel that:

No one in your family loved you or thought you were important or special? OR Your family didn't look out for each other, feel close to each other, or support each other?

Yes or No... If Yes, enter 1 _____

5. Did you often feel that:

You didn't have enough to eat, had to wear dirty clothes, and had no one to protect you? OR Your parents were too drunk or high to take care of you or take you to the doctor if you needed it?

Yes or No... If Yes, enter 1 _____

6. Were your parents ever separated or divorced?

Yes or No... If Yes, enter 1 _____

7. Were any of your parents or other adult caregivers:

Often pushed, grabbed, slapped, or had something thrown at them? OR Sometimes or often kicked, bitten, hit with a fist, or hit with something hard? OR Ever repeatedly hit over at least a few minutes or threatened with a gun or knife?

Yes or No... If Yes, enter 1 _____

8. Did you live with anyone who was a problem drinker or alcoholic, or who used street drugs?

Yes or No... If Yes, enter 1 _____

9. Was a household member depressed or mentally ill, or did a household member attempt suicide?

Yes or No... If Yes, enter 1 _____

10. Did a household member go to prison?

Yes or No... If Yes, enter 1 _____

ACE SCORE (Total "Yes" Answers): _____

The ACE Study revealed five main discoveries:

1. ACEs are common...nearly two-thirds (64%) of adults have at least one.

2. They cause adult onset of chronic disease, such as cancer and heart disease, as well as mental illness, violence and being a victim of violence.

3. ACEs don't occur alone...if you have one, there's an 87% chance that you have two or more.

4. The more ACEs you have, the greater the risk for chronic disease, mental illness, violence and being a victim of violence. People have an ACE score of 0 to 10. Each type of trauma counts as one, no matter how many times it occurs. You can think of an ACE score as a cholesterol score for childhood trauma. For example, people with an ACE score of 4 are twice as likely to be smokers and seven times more likely to be alcoholic. Having an ACE score of 4 increases the risk of emphysema or chronic bronchitis by nearly 400 percent, and suicide by 1200 percent. People with high ACE scores are more likely to be violent, to have more marriages, more broken bones, mor edrug prescriptions, more depression, and more autoimmune diseases. People with an ACE score of 6 or higher are at risk of their lifespan being shortened by 20 years.

5. ACEs are responsible for a big chunk of workplace absenteeism, and for costs in health care, emergency response, mental health, and criminal justice. So, the fifth finding from the ACE Study is that childhood adversity contributes to most of our major chronic health, mental health, economic health and social health issues.[iii]

As mentioned earlier, while the findings of this study are comprehensive they do not cover all types of adverse childhood experiences. You may have a score of 0 on the quiz and still have experienced one or more ACEs that are affecting your life.

Awareness Tool: The ACEs we have experienced growing up will continue to have negative impacts on the rest of our lives, until we resolve that trauma. RF

i "Fast Facts: Preventing Adverse Childhood Experiences" *Centers for Disease Control and Prevention.* (n.d.) https://www.cdc.gov/violenceprevention/aces/fastfact.html#:~:text=ACEs%20are%20common.,or%20mo re%20types%20of%20ACEs ii http://www.odmhsas.org/picis/TraningInfo/ACE.pdf iii "The Consequences of Childhood Trauma." *Bryon Clinic.* (n.d.) https://byronclinic.com/finding-your-ace-score/

WORKSHEET 3

List a few words that describe the negative consequences that have developed in each dimension of your life from impulsive, unhealthy decisions.

Example

1	Physical	1	Broken bones, arrested, sick, pain.

THE EIGHT DIMENSIONS OF WELLNESS		NEGATIVE CONSEQUENCES OF IMPULSIVE DECISIONS	
1	EMOTIONAL	1	
2	FINANCIAL	2	
3	SOCIAL	3	
4	SPIRITUAL	4	
5	OCCUPATIONAL	5	
6	PHYSICAL	6	
7	INTELLECTUAL	7	
8	ENVIRONMENTAL	8	

Examine how to reduce impulsive decision-making. What can you change?

WORKSHEET 4

List a few words that describe the positive consequences or rewards that can develop in each dimension of your life from balanced, calm, and healthy decisions.

Example

1	Physical	1	Physically fit, rested, peaceful, capable.

THE EIGHT DIMENSIONS OF WELLNESS		POSITIVE CONSEQUENCES OF BALANCED DECISIONS
1	EMOTIONAL	1
2	FINANCIAL	2
3	SOCIAL	3
4	SPIRITUAL	4
5	OCCUPATIONAL	5
6	PHYSICAL	6
7	INTELLECTUAL	7
8	ENVIRONMENTAL	8

Consider ways to make healthy choices based on facts rather than emotions.

WORKSHEET 5

The positive effects of Trauma-Informed approaches in your life.

THE KEY CONCEPTS OF TRAUMA-INFORMED CARE ARE:

1

2

3

WHAT ARE THE BENEFITS OF TRAUMA-INFORMED APPROACHES?

WHAT DOES TRAUMA-RESPONSIVE CARE PROVIDE?

WORKSHEET 6

Re-traumatization. Re-traumatization has a huge impact on our ability to heal. Answer the questions below.

"The Impact of Trauma in Personal Social Development"

◆ What is re-traumatization?

◆ How has your trauma contributed to unhealthy coping in life?

◆ What is a repeated negative trigger that re-traumatizes you?

◆ How often does a trauma trigger lead you to substance abuse?

◆ What are healthy ways to stop triggering re-traumatization in your life?

Read "An Autobiography In Five Chapters" on the next page.

AN AUTOBIOGRAPHY IN FIVE CHAPTERS

Chapter 1

I walk down the street.
There is a deep hole in the sidewalk.
I fall in.
I am lost...I am helpless.
It isn't my fault.
It takes forever to find a way out.

Chapter 2

I walk down the same street.
There is a deep hole in the sidewalk.
I pretend I don't see it.
I fall in, again.
I can't believe I am in this same place.
But it isn't my fault.
It still takes a long time to get out.

Chapter 3

I walk down the same street.
There is a deep hole in the sidewalk.
I see it is there.
I fall in...it's a habit...
But, my eyes are open.
I know where I am.
It is my fault.
I get out immediately.

Chapter 4

I walk down the same street.
There is a deep hole in the sidewalk.
I walk around it.

Chapter 5

I walk down a different street.

-Anonymous

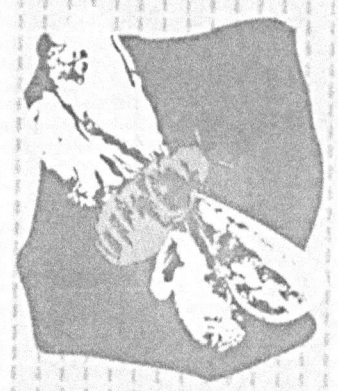

WORKSHEET 7

After reading "An Autobiography In Five Chapters," answer the questions below.

- Understanding Trauma

◆ How can this autobiography help you in your wellness journey?

◆ What did you learn from "An Autobiography In Five Chapters"?

◆ How can you apply this in your daily life?

NOTES:

Continue to Module 1 Quiz on the next page.

QUIZ ✦ MODULE 1

TRUE   **FALSE**

1   Awareness is important because when we are aware of the environment around us and inside of us we are able to make different choices and decisions.

2   General awareness and self-awareness have no effect on substance abuse recovery.

3   Self-awareness is important because it allows us to see why we might have an issue, how we are acting, and why we are acting that way.

4   Trauma can take various forms. We all have trauma because we have all had negative experiences in our lives.

5   Trauma is not prevalent in our lives; it does not comprise human potential and diminish life quality. Trauma does not have negative impacts on our lives.

6   A trigger will lead to the impulse; when that happens we cannot stop and make a choice. We have to make choices based on reactions and impulses.

7   ACEs are not linked to long-term health problems, mental illness, and drug or alcohol abuse.

8   We can choose to address and release our past trauma and reprogram to a positive mindset.

9   Trauma-Informed approach means speaking to the person and calling them "bad" or "broken."

10   A Trauma-Informed approach is important because with this approach we avoid re-traumatizing or blaming individuals for trying to manage their traumatic reactions.

SELF CHECK-IN — SCALE 0-10

Take an inventory of where you are. There are no rights or wrongs; this is a self-reflective check-in to see where you are doing well or where you want to improve. Rate statements below from 0 to 10.

1   I would like to improve awareness in my life.

2   I feel valuable.

3   I don't have much trauma in my life.

4   I allow myself to have feelings.

5   I do not make impulsive decisions often.

6   I am frequently re-traumatized and triggered.

7   I would like to work on a Trauma-Informed life approach.

8   I am open to releasing trauma.

9   I realize that repeated trauma cycles are not healthy.

10 I feel hopeful.

We all struggle, We can all heal. You are not alone.

MODULE JOURNAL

Optional Notes

You are the miracle You've been looking for.

QUIZ ✦ MODULE 1 (ANSWERS)

		TRUE	FALSE
1	Awareness is important because when we are aware of the environment around us and inside of us we are able to make different choices and decisions.	✓	
2	General awareness and self-awareness have no effect on substance abuse recovery.		✓
3	Self-awareness is important because it allows us to see why we might have an issue, how we are acting, and why we are acting that way.	✓	
4	Trauma can take various forms. We all have trauma because we have all had negative experiences in our lives.	✓	
5	Trauma is not prevalent in our lives; it does not comprise human potential and diminish life quality. Trauma does not have negative impacts on our lives.		✓
6	A trigger will lead to the impulse; when that happens we cannot stop and make a choice. We have to make choices based on reactions and impulses.		✓
7	ACEs are not linked to long-term health problems, mental illness, and drug or alcohol abuse.		✓
8	We can choose to address and release our past trauma and reprogram to a positive mindset.	✓	
9	Trauma-Informed approach means speaking to the person and calling them "bad" or "broken."		✓
10	A Trauma-Informed approach is important because with this approach we avoid re-traumatizing or blaming individuals for trying to manage their traumatic reactions.	✓	

MODULE 1 SUMMARY

1 COURSE TAKEAWAY POINT ONE

- 1.1. Awareness of Trauma. Awareness is important because when we are aware of the environment around us and inside of us we are able to make different choices and decisions. We have the ability to choose what happens in our lives.

2 COURSE TAKEAWAY POINT TWO

- 1.2. The Impact of Trauma. Unresolved trauma leads to addictions, manifesting in unhealthy patterns such as anger, negativity, depression, anxiety, drug and alcohol abuse, eating disorders, excessive gambling, self-harm, and suicide.

3 COURSE TAKEAWAY POINT THREE

- 1.3. Trauma-Informed and Trauma-Responsive Support. Understanding the physical, social, and emotional consequences of trauma is the first step in a Trauma-Informed approach. This allows the individual to be met where they are at and to heal and overcome their trauma.

1 YOUR TAKEAWAY POINT ONE

- 1.1. Awareness of Trauma.

2 YOUR TAKEAWAY POINT TWO

- 1.2. The Impact of Trauma.

3 YOUR TAKEAWAY POINT THREE

- 1.3. Trauma-Informed and Trauma-Responsive Support.

DT: UNDERSTANDING TRAUMA

DECONSTRUCTING TRAUMA
IN PERSONAL SOCIAL DEVELOPMENT

2. TRAUMA AND NEGATIVITY

Awareness Tool
Reaching out for assistance and support of our mental health takes courage and strength. We ALL need mental support. You are not alone!

TRAUMA AND NEGATIVITY

MODULE 2

DT Book Chapter 2: Identify the Addiction to Negativity.

What are Negative Thought Patterns?
Negative thought patterns are repeated unhealthy negative thoughts that damage our lives and alter the body's chemistry in a harmful way. Negativity affects us at a cellular level.

Have you ever found yourself unable to stop thinking negative thoughts? Negative thinking causes us to focus on the negative aspects of a situation rather than the positives. Negative thinking patterns can manifest as incorrect assumptions, unrealistic self-criticisms, irrational fears, unwanted and/or repetitive thoughts, anger, resentment, insecurity, chronic fatigue, burnout, low energy, depressive states, anxiousness, chronic continual illness, self-loathing, and sometimes even refusal to acknowledge the existence of external realities.

Many of us grew up with the message that we should not show our emotions, so we attempt to ignore or suppress them. These negative emotions poison and harm us.

We either internalize them (resulting in anger, resentment, depressive states, despair, and resignation), or we externalize them and blame, discount, or bully others. Negative thought patterns have a damaging impact on our physical, mental, emotional, and spiritual health.

Why is Recognizing Negative Thought Patterns Important?
Recognizing negative thought patterns is important because your thoughts and values can determine the way you see yourself and the world around you. Thoughts and beliefs that are grounded in pessimism can negatively impact your feelings, emotions, and mental health. These harmful perceptions are common issues that can contribute to the symptoms of mood and chronic disorders, including substance abuse. Negative thinking makes you feel bad about the world, about yourself, about the future. It contributes to low self-worth. It makes you feel like you're not effective in the world. Negative thinking is linked to addiction, depression, anxiety, chronic worry and obsessive-compulsive disorder (OCD).

What does Negative Thinking do to Your Body?
Negative thinking can cause extreme harm to the body, mind, and spirit. Our lifespan can actually be shortened by persistent stress. Negativity is one of many things in life that can develop into a habit. Denial, cynical thinking, and repeated criticism can build neural pathways in the brain that support depressive states and sadness that lead to addictions.

Why are we so Hyper-focused on the Negative Aspects of Existence?
We are so hyper-focused on negativity because it is all we know; it is what we are most familiar with. When your brain releases reward chemicals like dopamine, you experience elation.

These negative thoughts are frequently repeated and turn into habits because they "reward" us.

The issue is that unchecked negative thinking is a habit as well. An addiction develops when something is perceived as beneficial, even though it is harmful, by our brains. We are all addicted to negativity and chaos. We are trying to fulfill our own value and worth through other people, places, and things. We have become accustomed to getting our own way and thinking that we should have perfect conditions — not too hot, not too cold; rain, but not too much rain; no destruction from weather, et cetera.

We are each responsible for our own level of happiness, and we are each responsible for our own level of unhappiness. Stress and challenges will happen. The reason they happen is so we can learn, grow, and become stronger from the experience, not so we can adopt them as our identity and concede to suffering. The vibration that we perceive ourselves to be in is what will manifest! We can learn to be grateful instead of hateful.

Why do We Glorify Struggle and Conflict?
We glorify struggle and conflict because we are addicted to the chemicals the body releases when in a state of stress. We call the brain's reward centers "pleasure centers," so it makes sense that when someone is addicted to drugs or alcohol the brain lights up and makes them want more. We know about that kind of addiction. But you don't need drugs or alcohol to make a self-reinforcing addiction circuit in your brain. The beta-endorphin and dopamine pathways are also turned on by pain and negative emotions like self-pity, anger, and guilt. These pathways are lit up by chronic jaw pain or painful thoughts in the same way they are by drugs.

Because of this, we can get hooked on those feelings. In this case, the biological process is simple: pain and bad feelings turn on the brain's reward centers, which makes the person unconsciously addicted to those bad feelings.

What are Examples of Negative Patterns?
Polarization or Dichotomous Thinking, Emotional Reasoning, Overgeneralization, Labeling, Jumping to Conclusions, Mental Filtering, Fortune-Telling, Mind-Reading, Magnification or Catastrophizing, Inability to Be Wrong, Control Fallacies, Fairness Fallacies, Change Fallacies, Minimizing or Discounting, Personalization and Self Blame, and Imperatives.

What is Cognitive Distortion? Why is it Important?
Cognitive distortions are repeated harmful thought patterns and errors in thinking. "Distortion" is used because negative thinking often leads to skewed perceptions of the world and false assumptions.

Common cognitive distortions include thinking yourself unworthy of love or success, believing everyone hates you, blaming yourself for your parents' divorce, and other self-destructive beliefs. Cognitive distortions are not always self-deprecating, however. They can also be projected onto other people and the world around you, such as believing everyone is lying, blaming a person or institution for your personal problems, or obsessing over a partner's feelings towards you.

Cognitive distortions are important because they are dangerous and can create a lifetime of trauma, chaos, pain, negativity, and addiction.

Recognizing cognitive distortions is the first step toward eliminating them from our thinking. We have a better chance of preventing the negative thought pattern from becoming an unhealthy life pattern and spiraling into a larger mental health crisis if we recognize and deal with the issue at the earliest stages of its development.

Awareness Tool: Learning to spot and stop negative thoughts and attitudes can help you prevent negative outcomes.

What Habits Lead to Cognitive Distortion?
Habits that lead to Cognitive Distortions are: Overthinking: obsessively thinking about the same thing over and over. Rumination: focusing on shortcomings and errors rather than ways to make things better. Cynical Hostility: directing rage, distrust, condemnation, or contempt toward others. These emotions might be the result of insecurity, protection, and unresolved trauma and can lead to substance abuse.

We are all drawn to see the negative; it is learned behavior. Unless we put in constant conscious effort to see the positive, we will live in a negative state, invoking our fight-or-flight distress response. Living in this state has grave effects on our physical, mental, and spiritual health and well-being. By hanging onto negative emotions, we are punishing ourselves.

Learning to reframe our beliefs to reinforce the actions we want to keep is possible.

When we prioritize the belief that allows us to act in accordance with our values we are less likely to experience inner turmoil.

We can continue to dispute our negative beliefs and thoughts, replacing them with more positive and realistic ones. When we start confronting our negative views, we begin to notice how many of them are not true in our lives. Instead of assuming the worst, we may realize that we feel disappointed if we did not reach a certain goal, but also accept that we are learning and growing from our mistakes and setbacks.

It's okay to feel out of balance. It happens to all of us, especially in tumultuous situations. We have been taught to put a piece of tape over the "check engine" light. We have been taught to stuff down our emotions or we will be seen as weak, that nothing's wrong even when it is.

There is no greater strength than to see the uncomfortable and sit with it. Not drown or wallow, but just observe. It's okay to not be okay! What is the lesson? What can we learn?

When we are in pain, our suffering can be magnified by the fear that the pain will never end. When we are enjoying ourselves, the unfortunate reality is that nothing lasts forever.

How do we strike a balance between these shifts? We can learn to nurture the space between by not pulling toward or pushing away, allowing us to be fully present to every change in our lives. We spend so much energy on what we already know has a negative outcome.

Redirecting that energy, releasing what has happened in the past and moving to a new future, will change our lives. In this way, we learn to choose wisely where we put our energy and intentions.

What is Mindfulness? Why is it Important?
Mindfulness is the practice of being in the present moment without judgment, and it has been shown to help people in important ways, both mentally and physically. Mindfulness is the practice of remaining nonjudgmental, with heightened awareness of one's thoughts, emotions, and experiences from moment to moment.

Self-Awareness and Mindfulness You are the observer. You can watch your own thoughts and how one thought leads to another without reacting to any of them. When you separate yourself from the situation or even your own thoughts, you can see things clearly. People who know themselves well can look at their actions, feelings, and thoughts without ego or judgment. It's a rare skill because most of us interpret our situations based on how we feel. Self-awareness is important for us all because it allows us to evaluate our growth and effectiveness and change course if we need to.

Mindfulness is important because mindfulness protects us, our families, and our society. Mindfulness creates a safe space of support to heal and balance our past experiences and to build resilience. With the help of mindfulness, we can access our own awareness in a calm manner and avoid getting drawn into a never-ending stream of frantic thoughts.

Awareness Tool: Ask yourself daily: "What am I thinking, what am I speaking, what am I doing, what do I mean, how do I feel?"

WORKSHEET 1

What did you learn about negativity and trauma from this module?

What insight did you gain about how negativity and trauma reward us from this module?

What information in this module can assist you in understanding mindfulness in your own trauma healing journey?

What part of this module empowered you?

WORKSHEET 2

Awareness Tools in Negativity and Trauma

- *Awareness Tool: Repeated unhealthy, negative patterns can occur from our past trauma, leading to unhealthy coping patterns, which jeopardizes our ability to live healthy, happy lives. Pain and unpleasant emotions stimulate the brain's reward pathways, resulting in unconscious addiction to these negative feelings.*

- *Awareness Tool: The greatest show of strength is honesty with oneself. Rather than searching to fix or heal those around us, we start with what's inside — no illusions, no judgment, no ego, only facts. We are not our trauma; we are not our addictions.*

Negativity and Trauma.

- How has negativity contributed to unhealthy behavior patterns?

- How does negativity make you feel? How does it affect your thought processes?

Habits that lead to Cognitive Distortions are: Overthinking: obsessively thinking about the same thing over and over. Rumination: focusing on shortcomings and errors rather than ways to make things better. Cynical Hostility: directing rage, distrust, condemnation, or contempt toward others. These emotions might be the result of insecurity, protection, and unresolved trauma and can lead to unhealthy behavior patterns.

- List your repeated negative thoughts.

WORKSHEET 3

List a few words that describe the negative consequences that have developed in each dimension of your life from negative thoughts and thinking errors.

Example

| 1 | Occupational | 1 | I hate my job, I don't want to work, I'm not good enough. |

THE EIGHT DIMENSIONS OF WELLNESS		CONSEQUENCES OF NEGATIVE THOUGHTS
1	EMOTIONAL	1
2	FINANCIAL	2
3	SOCIAL	3
4	SPIRITUAL	4
5	OCCUPATIONAL	5
6	PHYSICAL	6
7	INTELLECTUAL	7
8	ENVIRONMENTAL	8

Examine how to reduce repeated negative thoughts and thinking errors. What tools can you use? What can you change?

WORKSHEET 4

List a few words that describe the positive consequences or rewards that can develop in each dimension of your life from positive thoughts and mindful thinking in your wellness journey.

Example

| 1 | Occupational | 1 | I like going to work, I feel accomplished and capable. |

THE EIGHT DIMENSIONS OF WELLNESS	CONSEQUENCES OF POSITIVE THOUGHTS
1 EMOTIONAL	1
2 FINANCIAL	2
3 SOCIAL	3
4 SPIRITUAL	4
5 OCCUPATIONAL	5
6 PHYSICAL	6
7 INTELLECTUAL	7
8 ENVIRONMENTAL	8

What was a decision you made that was based on emotions instead of facts? How did that end? What could you have done differently?

WORKSHEET 5

The positive effects of mindfulness-based approaches
in your life

MINDFULNESS IS:

**BENEFITS OF SELF-AWARENESS AND MINDFULNESS IN YOUR
TRAUMA HEALING JOURNEY:**

Notice what maybe helpful for you from this information.

At Sacred Sol Healing Institute, we have created the Deconstructing Trauma Program. This process connects positive behavior resilience and mindful behavior modification to mindfulness by applying the actions it takes to reprogram negative learned behavior and false identities. Below are a few examples for you to try.

Simple Mindfulness Practices

- When you are upset, pause, take a moment, ask yourself, "Why am I upset?" Whatever answer you come up with is okay – sit with it.

You don't have to act immediately. It will still be available at a later date and time! If it still matters at a later date and time it can be dealt with then.

- If you are unhappy, ask yourself why. "Why am I unhappy? Am I unhappy because of my expectations?" When we expect something we can be let down. Our expectations put limits not only on us, but the world around us. We can move forward with an idea rather than an expectation, because an idea is flexible and expectations are not.

- Clearing Breath: Inhale through the nose, let the belly and chest expand. Big exhale out the mouth, releasing pressure.

- Positive Breath: Inhale through the nose, drawing in positivity at the top of the head; exhale negativity out the mouth.

- We can use positive affirmations to reprogram negative behavior and emotional complications. For example, "I am capable, I am loved." When we add breath work and imagery with the affirma- tion, we will have a much deeper result.

SSHI Balancing Exercise:

Visualize positive light at the top of the head,
Inhale through the nose, drawing that light into your body,
Gently exhale that light out the mouth, letting it flow over your body toward the earth. Say, "I am capable, I am loved."
Repeat five times and see how you feel! Try it out!

To see our Mindful Behavior Modification Awareness Tools all in one convenient spot, download our Deconstructing Trauma Wellness Toolkit at deconstructing-trauma.com

What Habits Lead to Cognitive Distortion?

Habits that lead to Cognitive Distortion. In order to improve your mental health, you must recognize patterns within patterns. You might be bringing certain attitudes and mental practices into daily life that cause negative thought cycles. You can help yourself by becoming adept at spotting them as they happen and putting a stop to them before they take you somewhere bad.

1. Overthinking: It's important to consider all options before making a decision, but if your indecision about where to eat lunch is caused by feelings of insecurity and uncertainty, you may be engaging in a negative thought pattern. When you overthink something, you consider every decision you make from every angle imaginable and attempt to mentally simulate every possible result. At best, this can be draining, and at worst, it can be disastrous if your carefully thought-out predictions are proven to be false. Limit your thinking to avoid overthinking. Set and adhere to deadlines for yourself when making decisions. For a healthy way to clear your mind of some of those extra thoughts, consider yoga, a good workout, or doing breathing exercises.

2. Self-criticism: Self-reflection and self-awareness can be lovely things, but they can also be devastating if your thought process is clouded by negativity and despair. Do you frequently focus on shortcomings and errors rather than opportunities for improvement? A cyclical pattern known as negative ruminating causes you to project your flaws onto your imagined future and convinces you that things will only get worse. When you initially become aware of yourself becoming fixated on negative thoughts, break the cycle by doing something else. Avoid spending too much time alone with your thoughts. Read a book, watch a movie, engage in a hobby, or speak with a friend (but don't just use these activities as a convenient way to get rid of your bad thoughts). Don't use food or alcohol as distractions. Intoxication and overeating can make things worse.

3. Hostile Mindset: Cynical hostility is a mental attitude in which one harbors resentment, mistrust, condemnation, or contempt for others. These emotions might be the result of insecurity, projection, or unfinished business. Maintaining a network of support is challenging when you view other people as inherently harmful, evil, or unreliable. Such a hostile attitude has been linked in studies to high blood pressure and heart disease. Empathy can counter cynical hostility. Try to look at a situation from all angles rather than automatically assuming distrust. Look for ways to frame events in a cooperative rather than a competitive way.

Why do the following behaviors manifest?

Example 1: *Bully Behavior.* He is a bully because he was bullied and beat up at a time when he couldn't defend himself. So, he has adopted a way of coping, his protection and defense mechanism is diminishing people to make himself feel bigger and safer. This is not actually helping him be safe but it has become his altered sense of security. It is the only way he knows how to operate; it is based on fear. He is looking to find his value and self-worth through harming others because that's all he knows.

Example 2: *Over-giver Behavior.* He had such a big heart and wants to help everyone but does not know his limits or when he should balance so he continues to give until it comprises him. People in his life will continue to take, because he doesn't know how to stop offering. He cannot stop this runaway cycle because he is looking to find his self-worth and value through others rather than himself because that's all he knows.

Both examples are using external situations to attempt solve an internal disfunction.

Solution Example 1: We can definitely work through the fear and anger to release all that pain and suffering so his value and self-worth will not come from hurting others. It would be so much healthier for him and everyone around him.

Solution Example 2: We can definitely work through the fear and self-doubt to release all that pain and suffering so his value and self-worth will not come from giving to others until he hurt himself. It would be so much healthier for him and everyone around him.

Examples 1 and 2 both display inappropriate, unhealthy interactions because of their trauma from past experiences. Even though their behavior is inappropriate and dangerous for all involved, they are acting appropriately for their level of trauma. The solution is to unwind, and release the trauma that has caused the misguided behavior that attempts to keep them safe. As we begin to resolve and release the trauma that has caused this behavior, the behavior will shift as the threat that caused the original unstable behavior is no longer significant. In this way they can both move forward with happiness, peace, and joy, sure of self and safe within.

> **Awareness Tool:**
> *Negativity weighs heavy... If you feel like something's too much it's because it is! RF*

This information is an awareness tool. We are not supposed to handle all the things that come to us. No one would expect you to pack four cars around on your back, so why do we think we are supposed to keep handling all the things that happen without unloading some of them first?

We are all drawn to see the negative; it is learned behavior. Unless we put in constant conscious effort to see the positive, we will live in a negative state, invoking our fight-or-flight distress response. Living in this state has grave effects on our physical, mental, and spiritual health and well-being. By hanging onto negative emotions, we are punishing ourselves.

Learning to reframe our beliefs to reinforce the actions we want to keep *is* possible. When we prioritize the belief that allows us to act in accordance with our values we are less likely to experience inner turmoil.

*Try this exercise: Visualize 10 balloons. The balloons represent our beliefs. Begin to inflate your balloons with the positive beliefs that you would like to incorporate into your life.

Examples: Inflate: Love, Safety, Peace, Joy, Happiness, Independence, Financial Safety, et cetera.

The negative damaging thoughts will slowly deflate as you focus on your positive top priorities. This awareness and action allows you to reprogram negative belief systems.

Examples: Deflate: Anxiousness, Stress, Anger, Sadness, Hopelessness, Depressed feelings, Financial Struggle, et cetera.

We can continue to dispute our beliefs and thoughts, replacing them with more positive and realistic ones. When we start confronting our negative views, we begin to notice how many of them are not true in our lives. Instead of assuming the worst, we may realize that we feel disappointed if we did not reach a certain goal, but also accept that we are learning and growing from our mistakes and setbacks.

It's okay to feel out of balance. It happens to all of us, especially in tumultuous situations. We have been taught to put a piece of tape over the "check engine" light. We have been taught to stuff down our emotions or we will be seen as weak, that nothing's wrong even when it is. There is no greater strength than to see the uncomfortable and sit with it. Not drown or wallow, but just observe. *It's okay to not be okay! What is the lesson? What can we learn?*

We can sit with it, be aware of it, observe it, allow it ... no judgment, no ego. By allowing the imbalance, we find balance.

By recognizing our own weaknesses, flaws, and wounds, we can start to heal. As we take responsibility for our actions, we are able to reprogram negativity and reduce chaos, leading us to happiness and joy.

> **Awareness Tool:**
> *The greatest show of strength is honesty with oneself. Rather than searching to fix or heal those around us, we start with what's inside – no illusions, no judgment, no ego, only facts. RF*

When we are in pain, our suffering can be magnified by the fear that the pain will never end. When we are enjoying ourselves, the unfortunate reality is that nothing lasts forever. How do we strike a balance between these shifts? We can learn to nurture the space between by not pulling toward or pushing away, allowing us to be fully present to every change in our lives.

We spend so much energy on what we already know has a negative outcome. Redirecting that energy, releasing what has happened in the past and moving to a new future, will change our lives. In this way, we learn to choose wisely where we put our energy and intentions. They are truly powerful tools.

How do we unload in a good way? How do we achieve this?
Through awareness and mindfulness.

WORKSHEET 6

Cognitive distortions refer to patterns of thinking that are not objective realities and can lead to inaccurate perceptions and interpretations of information. Answer the questions below.

"Cognitive Distortions in Personal Social Development"

◆ What are cognitive distortions?

◆ How have cognitive distortions contributed to unhealthy behavior patterns?

◆ What is a repeated cognitive distortion that triggers and re-traumatizes you?

◆ How often does a cognitive distortion lead you to unhealthy behavior patterns?

◆ What are healthy ways to stop cognitive distortions in your life?

Read "What Causes Conflict in Your Life" on the next page.

• ADDICTION TO NEGATIVE THOUGHT PATTERNS

What Causes Conflict in Your Life

Anger · Neglect · Mental Abuse · Physical Abuse · Alcohol

Drugs · Criticism · Sex · Relationships · Arguing · Anxiety

Victim · Hate · Co-Dependence · Annoyances · Irritable

Addiction · Damaging Core Beliefs · Gambling · Death · Food · DHS

Lack of Self-Respect · Lies · Sexual Assault · Lack of Self-Worth

Spiritual Abuse · Abandonment · Child Abuse · Environment

Bullying · Dissociation · Belittling · Shame · Not Being Forgiven

Pride · Poor Decision-Making · Downgrading · Comparing

Resentment · Self-Blame · Ego · Lack Of Confidence · Suicide

Righteous Religion · People Pleasing · Recklessness · Labeling

No Self-Love · Depression · Lack of Approval · Boredom

Isolation · Self-Medicating · Lack of Respect · Loneliness · Spite

Lack of Responsibility · Wrath · Vengeance · Jealousy · Greed

Perfectionist · Excuses · Envy · Rage · Selfishness · Judging

Adopting Others' Opinions · Cheating · Assumptions · Bills

Self-Sabotage · Meddling · Guilt Frustration · Family · Finances

Negligence · Disappointment · Lack of Work · False Identity

Bad Choices · Assumptions · Disease · Suffering · Trauma

Negativity weighs heavy on us. If each one of these words weighed
5 pounds it would be over 400 pounds...way too much to carry.
That weight transfers to our body, mind, and sprit.
Release the negative, find positivity and hope. You are not alone!

WORKSHEET 7

After reading "What Causes Conflict in Your Life," answer the questions below.

- Negativity and Trauma

◆ How can awareness of what causes conflict help you in your unhealthy behavior patterns?

◆ What did you learn from reading What Causes Conflict in Your Life?

◆ How can you apply this in your daily life?

NOTES:

Continue to Module 2 Quiz on the next page.

- ADDICTION TO NEGATIVE THOUGHT PATTERNS

QUIZ ✳ MODULE 2

TRUE   FALSE

1 Negative thought patterns are repeated unhealthy negative thoughts that damage our lives, and alter the body's chemistry in a harmful way. Negativity affects us at a cellular level.

2 Negative thinking is linked to addiction, depression, anxiety, chronic worry and OCD.

3 Thoughts and beliefs that are grounded in pessimism do not negatively impact your feelings, emotions, mental health, or substance abuse.

4 Cognitive distortions are not dangerous; they do not create a lifetime of trauma, chaos, pain, negativity, and addiction. They help us feel safe.

5 Denial, cynical thinking, and repeated criticism can build neural pathways in the brain that support depressive states and sadness that lead to addictions.

6 You can watch your own thoughts and how one thought leads to another, but you have to react to them. Separating yourself from the situation or even your own thoughts doesn't help at all.

7 Negativity is not one of many things in life that can develop into a habit.

8 Mindfulness creates a safe space of support to heal and balance our past experiences, building resilience.

9 You need drugs or alcohol to make a self-reinforcing addiction circuit in your brain.

10 We are not responsible for our own level of happiness, and we are not responsible for our own level of unhappiness.

SELF CHECK-IN — SCALE 0-10

Take an inventory of where you are. There are no rights or wrongs; this is a self-reflective check-in to see where you are doing well or where you want to improve. Rate statements below from 0 to 10.

1   I would like to reduce negative thinking.

2   I feel safe.

3   I don't have many unhealthy habits.

4   I allow myself to think before I act.

5   I do not have urges to use substances.

6   I am frequently focused on the negative aspects of life.

7   I would like to work on a mindful life approach.

8   I am open to releasing cognitive distortions.

9   I realize that repeated negative thoughts are not healthy.

10   I feel strong.

We all struggle, We can all heal. You are not alone.

MODULE JOURNAL
Optional Notes

You are the miracle You've been looking for.

QUIZ ✳ MODULE 2 (ANSWERS)

		TRUE	FALSE
1	Negative thought patterns are repeated unhealthy negative thoughts that damage our lives, and alter the body's chemistry in a harmful way. Negativity affects us at a cellular level.	✓	
2	Negative thinking is linked to addiction, depression, anxiety, chronic worry and OCD.	✓	
3	Thoughts and beliefs that are grounded in pessimism do not negatively impact your feelings, emotions, mental health, or substance abuse.		✓
4	Cognitive distortions are not dangerous; they do not create a lifetime of trauma, chaos, pain, negativity, and addiction. They help us feel safe.		✓
5	Denial, cynical thinking, and repeated criticism can build neural pathways in the brain that support depressive states and sadness that lead to addictions.	✓	
6	You can watch your own thoughts and how one thought leads to another, but you have to react to them. Separating yourself from the situation or even your own thoughts doesn't help at all.		✓
7	Negativity is not one of many things in life that can develop into a habit.		✓
8	Mindfulness creates a safe space of support to heal and balance our past experiences, building resilience.	✓	
9	You need drugs or alcohol to make a self-reinforcing addiction circuit in your brain.		✓
10	We are not responsible for our own level of happiness, and we are not responsible for our own level of unhappiness.		✓

MODULE 2 SUMMARY

1   **COURSE TAKEAWAY POINT ONE**

- 2.1. Negativity and Trauma. Negative thinking makes you feel bad about the world, yourself, and the future. It contributes to low self-worth, trauma, and addiction, making you feel like you're not effective in the world.

2   **COURSE TAKEAWAY POINT TWO**

- 2.2. Addiction to Negative Thought Patterns. Cognitive distortions are important because they are dangerous and can create a lifetime of trauma, chaos, pain, negativity, and addiction. Negative habits that lead to cognitive distortions.

3   **COURSE TAKEAWAY POINT THREE**

- 2.3. Mindfulness and Trauma Healing. Mindfulness is the practice of remaining nonjudgmental with heightened awareness of one's thoughts, emotions, and experiences from moment to moment. Mindfulness can help us understand and meet our needs instead of using unhealthy coping patterns to check out.

1   **YOUR TAKEAWAY POINT ONE**

- 2.1. Negativity and Trauma.

2   **YOUR TAKEAWAY POINT TWO**

- 2.2. Addiction to Negative Thought Patterns.

3   **YOUR TAKEAWAY POINT THREE**

- 2.3. Mindfulness and Trauma Healing.

DECONSTRUCTING TRAUMA
IN PERSONAL SOCIAL DEVELOPMENT

3. DAILY TRIGGERS-
LEARNED BEHAVIOR

Awareness Tool

An emotional trigger is anything – a memory, an experience, or an event – that causes a strong emotional reaction, regardless of your current state of mind. Observing the circumstances under which you experience intense emotions is crucial for identifying your triggers.

DAILY TRIGGERS-LEARNED BEHAVIOR

MODULE 3

DT Book Chapter 3. Understand Daily Triggers and Learned Behavior

What is a Trigger? Why are they Important?
A trigger, also known as a stressor, is an event or circumstance that may result in a negative emotional response. A trigger is a stimulus that can bring back an unpleasant memory, emotion, or symptom.

We generally go through a range of emotions every day, including excitement, unease, frustration, joy, and disappointment. These frequently correspond with specific events, like attending a meeting with your supervisor, running into an ex-partner or friend, remembering the anniversary of a loss or traumatic event, hearing terrifying news, having too much on your plate, feeling overwhelmed, experiencing conflict in the family, ending a relationship, spending too much time alone, receiving a large bill, et cetera.

Depending on your state of mind and the situational factors, your reaction to these events may differ. We don't talk enough about triggers in the ongoing conversation about mental health.

Most frequently, the topic of conversation centers on what transpires after being triggered, which is the point at which the problem is most difficult to resolve. It can be more empowering and efficient to recognize triggers, understand them, and take steps to resolve, and or avoid, them.

Understanding Triggers. Events that serve as triggers are highly subjective and can look very different depending on the person. Heavy breathing, jaw clenching, upset stomach, trembling, chest pain, dizziness, crying, and sweating are all physiological responses that can be triggered.

An emotional reaction can be set off by a thought, such as, "I am being attacked, blamed, controlled, smothered, disrespected, rejected, betrayed, criticized, ignored, unwanted, judged, and/or having my beliefs challenged." Many different emotions, including anger, hurt, overwhelmed, powerlessness, helplessness, fear, anxiousness, sadness, unloved, weakness, and pain, can result from experiencing a trigger.

Tackling these emotions can be incredibly challenging and can have serious consequences for our mental health. The consequences of a person's emotional reaction to something can range from mildly disruptive to extremely dangerous, such as acts of violence.

An individual's susceptibility to and intensity of an emotional reaction to a trigger may increase significantly, relative to those of an individual in the same situation who is not exposed to the trigger.

Some people may also lack insight into their reactions and have impaired judgment after experiencing a trigger, which can lead to substance abuse.

Triggers are important because as we begin to recognize what affects us in our daily lives, we are able to mitigate, or lessen, negativity, pain, addiction, and trauma. As we resolve triggers and negativity in our lives we are able to live in balance, happiness, and peace.

What are Negative and Positive Learned Behaviors? Why are they Important?
Negative learned behavior develops as a result of experience. Understanding negative learned behavior is important because by identifying that we have learned a particular behavior we are able to understand that negative behavior equals negative results.

We have a choice; we are not helpless and can take action to change this.

Negative experiences create blockages over time; they become tangled with other experiences and blockages, building layers of pain, trauma, and suffering that lead to extreme discomfort and addiction.

So, how do we untangle these blockages? It is a matter of unwinding, releasing, and peeling back the layers one at a time. As we begin to understand the purpose of our experiences, we are able to start the healing process. It is like peeling back the layers of an onion.

It is awesome when the top layer is released, but that does not untangle all the layers at once. It takes a bit of work to untangle reactive learned behavior, especially when we are strongly set in negative patterns.

We will learn how to release these blockages through awareness and action! So how does positive behavior develop?

Positive learned behavior develops as a result of experience. If we have been guided and supported through a challenging experience, we adopt a positive learned behavior trait because of this experience.

Example: If you are told you CAN learn to accomplish your goal when trying something new, you will most likely be empowered and begin to believe that you can accomplish anything you set your mind to.

This then becomes part of a positive belief system that carries you through a successful, fulfilling life. Understanding positive learned behavior is important because by identifying that we have learned a particular behavior we are able to understand that positive behavior equals positive results. We have a choice; we are not helpless and can take action to continue positivity and healthy choices in our lives.

What is Negative Talk of Others? Why it is Important?
Negative talk of others is when we put people down, instead of speaking kindly or saying nothing at all. Negative talk of others brings people's mood down; it reflects pessimism, anxiousness, and general sense of distrust. Negative talk of others is important because it is "a thinly disguised cry for help, a need to feel respected, loved, and in control." People talk negative of others because they are not happy with themselves. This comes from past trauma, and negative learned behavior patterns that then form negative habits.

Awareness Tool: Constant exposure to negativity can significantly deplete our positivity, causing us to either become negative (doubtful, anxious, and distrustful), indifferent, uncaring, or even cruel.

What is Negative Self-Talk? How do we Reduce it? Why is it Important?
Negative Self-talk is constantly finding fault in yourself. Nothing is ever good enough. We all have an inner critic. This voice can often be more harmful than helpful, especially when buried in excessive negativity. Reduce negative self-talk by becoming aware of it, wanting to stop it, and taking action to implement tools and techniques that reprogram negative learned behavior.

Negative self-talk is important because it can affect us in damaging ways, including mental health challenges, depressive states, anxiousness, toxic stress, insomnia, anger, addiction, hopelessness, despair, unhealthy relationships, and more.

Awareness Tool: Negative self-talk is thinking that undermines our ability to make positive shifts in our lives. Negative self-talk is stressful and limits our success, self-confidence, and potential.

Why do We Feel like No One Listens, or that No One Cares?
We may feel like no one listens or cares because each of us is operating with a different set of expectations. Even though someone might be listening, we feel that they aren't if we don't receive the response we think is correct, in the way we think is correct.

Our expectations are based on our prior experiences. Others will have different experiences and therefore have different expectations. It is inappropriate to base the value of a relationship on a difference of opinion. We each have our own needs.

Why Are We Always Giving More Than Receiving? Why Do We Feel Unappreciated?

Many times, we feel unappreciated because we are giving too much in order to feel loved and accepted. We may do way more than is needed to show how much we care. Frantically running from one thing to the next is an inappropriate way of seeking love and acceptance. This behavior puts others in a bad position because no matter how much they appreciate us, it is never enough.

This behavior also puts us at risk because we are doing way too much and are completely overextended, causing toxic stress, addiction, and physical and emotional suffering. When we begin to give ourselves the love and acceptance we are looking for, we do not need constant validation from others. We can reduce the number of things we are doing for others and allow balance and joy in our lives.

Why Do We React Instead of Respond When We are Not in Danger?

We react instead of respond because we feel threatened physically, mentally, emotionally or spiritually. This threat comes from past experience, and because we have not resolved traumatic past experiences we will still have the same reaction as when the threat was real and imminent. A reaction (quick and aggressive behavior) is part of fight-or-flight. A response (compassion for both parties) is a choice we have thought about.

Awareness Tool: Critical thoughts of self and others keep us in a constant state of fight-or-flight. We can begin to examine situations that upset us to determine if the threat is real or perceived. With this perspective, we can change our lives drastically by reducing stress, anger, and addiction.

What is a Real Threat? What is a Perceived Threat?

A real threat is a bear chasing us; a perceived threat is someone taking our parking spot. We can begin to examine situations that upset us to determine if the threat is real or perceived.

Because of our traumatic experiences, the hypothalamus shuts off — we stay in fight-or-flight and are unable to make cohesive, cognizant choices. We become numb and continue to look for chaos because it is the most familiar place we know how to operate from. We are unable to shift from this pattern and that creates more chaos. In order to break the cycle, we can reprogram the brain to release this damage and reset, creating a different storage of memories. Once the brain has reset, so will the body.

We will not continue to have a visceral body reaction once the brain resolves the trauma. There are many tools that allow us to reprogram to a space of safety, but the breath is by far the most effective! The breath can balance the central nervous system. When the central nervous system is balanced, this activates the parasympathetic central nervous system, which allows peace, safety, happiness, and joy to be received.

When we have activated the parasympathetic nervous system we have deactivated fight-or-flight (the sympathetic nervous system). They cannot both be activated at the same time. We are either in drive or reverse. We are either safe or unsafe.

The reality we perceive ourselves to be in is the truth and reality we will live in. We are used to chaos and addiction. We have the ability to change that.Whatever we are most familiar with, we will automatically go back to.

WORKSHEET 1

◆ What did you learn about daily triggers and learned behavior from this module?

◆ What understanding did you gain from this module about how negative dialogues feed the cycle of trauma?

◆ What information in this module helped you understand how trauma cycles create automatic trauma responses in our daily lives?

◆ What part of this module empowered you?

WORKSHEET 2

Awareness Tools in Daily Triggers-Learned Behavior.

- *Awareness Tool: Many times, the world around us, accompanied with our past traumatic experiences, will send us into a space of unsafety. Learning the skills and tools to return yourself to a state of safety can change your life.*

- *Awareness Tool: People who are truly content rarely engage in negative talk. It is not appealing for them to talk negatively.*

- *Awareness Tool: We can change our experience and release the negative patterns that have been a continued cycle in our lives.*

How Trauma Triggers Lead to Unhealthy Patterns.

- How have trauma triggers contributed to unhealthy patterns?

- How do triggers make you feel? How do they affect your thought processes?

List your trauma triggers.

WORKSHEET 3

List a few words that describe the negative consequences that have developed in each dimension of your life from your negative dialogues that have fed the trauma cycle.

Example

1	Social	1	"No one likes me"; "I'm not good enough"; awkward communicating.

THE EIGHT DIMENSIONS OF WELLNESS		NEGATIVE CONSEQUENCES OF MY NEGATIVE DIALOGUES	
1	EMOTIONAL	1	
2	FINANCIAL	2	
3	SOCIAL	3	
4	SPIRITUAL	4	
5	OCCUPATIONAL	5	
6	PHYSICAL	6	
7	INTELLECTUAL	7	
8	ENVIRONMENTAL	8	

Examine how to reduce negative dialogues.
What can you change?

WORKSHEET 4

List a few words that describe the positive consequences or rewards that can develop in each dimension of your life from positive dialogue. Changing your dialogue can contribute to healing cycles of trauma.

Example

| 1 | Social | 1 | Connect with positive friends & events; have fun. |

THE EIGHT DIMENSIONS OF WELLNESS		POSITIVE CONSEQUENCES OF POSITIVE DIALOGUES	
1	EMOTIONAL	1	
2	FINANCIAL	2	
3	SOCIAL	3	
4	SPIRITUAL	4	
5	OCCUPATIONAL	5	
6	PHYSICAL	6	
7	INTELLECTUAL	7	
8	ENVIRONMENTAL	8	

Identify a self-critical dialogue in your life and how you can positively rephrase it.

Continue on to Self-Critical Thought Records.

• HOW NEGATIVE DIALOGUES FEED THE TRAUMA CYCLE

Record a childhood self-critical thought pattern.

SELF-CRITICAL THOUGHT RECORD

SITUATION-TRIGGER:

EMOTIONS:

PHYSICAL SENSATIONS:

SELF-CRITICAL THOUGHTS:

ALTERNATIVE POSITIVE THOUGHTS:

HOW COULD THIS HAVE CHANGED YOUR OUTCOME:

SELF-CRITICAL THOUGHT RECORD

SITUATION-TRIGGER:

EMOTIONS:

PHYSICAL SENSATIONS:

SELF-CRITICAL THOUGHTS:

ALTERNATIVE POSITIVE THOUGHTS:

HOW COULD THIS HAVE CHANGED YOUR OUTCOME:

Types Of Triggers

Triggers can manifest in many different ways and are strongly influenced by past experiences. Extreme distress, conflict, illness, and other negative outcomes may result from such triggers.

External triggers *are people, places, things, activities, and situations.*
Example: When I quit drinking alcohol, I had to stay away from places that carried alcohol and people who drank. It was a trigger for me to think about it, let alone see or smell it. My physical body would shake like I was going through withdrawals all over again.
Resolution: I resolved this by not being around alcohol at all until the severity of the trigger reduced (1-2 years).

Internal triggers *are feelings or thoughts that people have before or during a situation.*
Example: I was triggered and felt abandoned when my spouse avoided me in order to avoid conflict. I would explode in anger because I had severe abandonment issues from childhood trauma.
Resolution: I resolved this by telling my spouse how avoiding conversation made me feel because of my past, and he assured me that he would not leave me.

Trauma triggers *are negative emotional/physical responses to a previous threatening situation.*
Example: Being in close proximity to the hospital where I endured a traumatic hospitalization. Every time I passed it, I was "retraumatized" and reminded of my hospitalization.
Resolution: After being repeatedly triggered, I decided to avoid the hospital by walking in a different direction.

Symptom triggers *are negative experiences that arise from other symptoms.*
Example: A lack of or reduced amount of sleep triggers my anxiousness.
Resolution: In this situation, I quickly address any sleep disruption with meditation and breathwork. This brings me back to peace and a resting heart rate, allowing restful sleep.

*Understanding the emotions we encounter on a daily basis is
the first step in learning how to deal with triggers. RF*

A memory is easier to recall the more sensory information that has been stored. The brain frequently stores sensory stimuli from a traumatic event in memory. We can still link the triggers to the trauma even if we come across the same stimuli in a different setting.

For example: I may be shopping in a mall and smell the same cologne I smelled when I was beaten years before. If I have not resolved this trauma, the very faintest scent of that cologne can bring me back to the same trauma I was experiencing in that moment twenty years ago. My body can elicit a trauma response from my sense of smell. It transports me back there and I begin flinching, sweating, and breathing heavily. *True story.*

According to Good Therapy, "In some cases, a sensory trigger can cause an emotional reaction before a person realizes why they are upset. Habit formation also plays a strong role in triggering. People tend to do the same things in the same way. Following the same patterns saves the brain from having to make decisions."[19]

This is where habits and awareness come in. We all build habits into our daily lives (i.e. driving a certain way to work, eating at particular places, et cetera), because it is comfortable and efficient. Becoming aware of our patterns, and what we are thinking and feeling while engaging in them, allows us to make changes that reduce the severity of triggers.

Awareness Tool:
The five senses are frequently the source of emotional triggers, so pay attention to what you see, hear, smell, taste, and touch as these could cause an emotion or a behavioral reaction.

Awareness Tool:
Triggers can teach us how to manage our reactions before they become problematic. We can stop triggers. Good emotional health requires knowing and managing your emotional triggers.

So, how do we resolve these triggers and habits?

Means of Dealing with Triggers and Difficult Circumstances

There is a wide range of responses one can take. Methods have been developed to prevent, delay, or lessen the intensity of an emotional response to a triggering event. We all have the opportunity to learn from our experiences. Different coping strategies may be effective for various stimuli and emotions.

Become aware of unhealthy coping skills such as violence, uncontrolled anger, emotional, psychological, sexual, or financial abuse, making justifications for harmful behavior, self-harm, or the emergence of bad behavioral compulsions.

Learn to recognize: Take into account your responses to previous triggers; who or what was involved; and where, when, and why they occurred. To avoid a repeat of the situation, look for patterns and obvious warning signs of risk. Try tracing the source of these emotions by recalling previous experiences that gave rise to the feelings you are currently experiencing.

Develop a strategy: Develop a strategy to deal with emotional outbursts and triggering events. You may want to talk to loved ones or your treatment team to let them know how they can best help you when you are experiencing triggers. Be sure to carefully address triggers that occur repeatedly, as the emotional reaction may become more intense with each subsequent occurrence of the trigger.

Consider a problem-solving approach: Address the source of your stress or begin taking steps to alleviate it.

Consider emotion-focused positive action: If you can't avoid a trigger, try an emotion-focused positive action to reduce its impact. Meditation reduces stress, anxiousness, and depressive states.

Communicate through the trigger: If someone is triggering you, talk to them about it. Most of the time, someone who triggers another person does not mean to do so. Talk to them about your trigger and how it affects you to clear up confusion. Consider possible solutions together, talking in a calm, open, and understanding way. It may be best to establish clear boundaries if the person who is triggering you isn't able to show compassion or understanding.

Trauma-Specific Therapy: Certain therapies can reduce triggers. Cognitive behavior therapy and emotionally-focused therapy help reduce trauma triggers.

Reasonable Thought Check: It can be helpful to "reality check" one's thoughts to determine how plausible they are in order to prevent an unwarranted escalation of emotions. This can help reduce the intensity of one's thoughts and feelings.

Reasonable Thought Check Options:
1 Verification of the facts: Think about the facts and ask yourself if they support your interpretation.
2 Recognize thought distortions: Identify inaccurate ways of thinking, perceiving, or believing something.
3 Reprogram: Shift your default negative thoughts to positive ones.
4 Proportionality: Ask yourself if the response is out of proportion to the triggering event.

Trigger warnings: Trigger warnings can help you avoid content that might upset you, especially content about suicide or violence. At the beginning of an article, TV show or film, sometimes a trigger warning is given.

Personal Health Care: Personal health care or self-care can assist in prioritizing mental health and help you resist triggers. Talk to a loved one, friend, or licensed therapist. Mindfulness, meditation, deep breathing, and journaling may help.

We can learn from our triggers even though controlling them is hard. We can use what we learn to prevent retriggering. Though it's challenging, experience can teach us how to better manage our reactions. We must consider both the trigger and what we can do to resolve it.

Downplaying the significance of the trigger or ignoring the importance of taking preventative measures is detrimental; instead, we can concentrate on what we can do to avoid being triggered in the first place. We have the ability to prevent and solve the problems that cause triggers! One of the most important aspects of emotional health is being aware of the factors that can set off your negative emotions, as well as the strategies you can use to manage them.

WORKSHEET 5

How Trauma Triggers Lead to Unhealthy Patterns.

LIST TYPES OF TRIGGERS AND HOW THEY CAN LEAD TO UNHEALTHY PATTERNS:

LIST WAYS OF DEALING WITH TRIGGERS AND DIFFICULT CIRCUMSTANCES:

WORKSHEET 6

"Automatic Trauma Responses" are created from repeated cycles of trauma. Answer the questions below.

"Automatic Trauma Responses in Daily Life"

◆ What happens to your body and mind when you feel threatened?

◆ When do you automatically want to reach for unhealthy coping mechanisms?

◆ What is a sound that makes you feel like you are in danger?

◆ What makes you feel uncomfortable or threatened, physically and mentally?

◆ What are healthy ways to feel safe and balanced in your life?

Read "10 Tips To Boost Your Mental Health" on the next page.

10 Tips To Boost Your Mental Health

- Connect with others
- Move your body
- Talk to someone
- Listen to music
- Meditate
- Schedule downtime
- Eat whole foods
- Reset when you can
- Practice setting boundaries
- Get help if you need it

WORKSHEET 7

After reading "10 Tips to Boost Your Mental Health," answer the questions below.

- Daily Triggers — Learned Behavior

◆ How can awareness of daily triggers and negative learned behaviors help you in your wellness journey?

◆ What did you learn from reading 10 Tips to Boost Your Mental Health?

◆ How can you apply this in your daily life?

NOTES:

Continue to Module 3 Quiz on the next page.

• HOW NEGATIVE DIALOGUES FEED THE TRAUMA CYCLE

QUIZ ✳ MODULE 3

TRUE   FALSE

1 A trigger, also known as a stressor, is an event or circumstance that does not result in a negative emotional response. A trigger never brings back unpleasant memories, emotions, or symptoms.

2 Negative learned behavior develops as a result of negative experiences.

3 People talk negatively about others because they are happy with themselves. They have not had past trauma or negative experiences.

4 People may lack insight into their reactions and have impaired judgment after experiencing a trigger, which can lead to substance abuse.

5 Even though someone might be listening, we feel that they aren't if we don't receive the response we think is correct, in the way we think is correct.

6 We never become numb and continue to look for chaos because it is the most familiar place we know how to operate from. We always release the patterns that create more chaos.

7 The reality we perceive ourselves to be in is never the truth and reality we will live in.

8 Positive learned behavior develops as a result of positive experiences.

9 Many times, we feel unappreciated because we are giving too much in order to feel loved and accepted.

10 The world around us is not filled with our past traumatic experiences; it doesn't send us into a space of unsafety. We don't need skills and tools to return ourselves to a state of safety.

SELF CHECK-IN — SCALE 0-10

Take an inventory of where you are. There are no rights or wrongs; this is a self-reflective check-in to see where you are doing well or where you want to improve. Rate statements below from 0 to 10.

1   I would like to reduce trauma triggers in my life.

2   I feel emotionally stable.

3   I don't have much stress in my life.

4   I have more negative experiences than positive.

5   I know I can accomplish my goals.

6   I don't talk negatively about others.

7   I would like to talk more positively about myself.

8   I do not feel appreciated.

9   I am always overextended and helping others.

10 I am in a state of panic and anxiety frequently.

We all struggle, We can all heal. You are not alone.

MODULE JOURNAL

You are the miracle You've been looking for.

QUIZ ✳ MODULE 3 (ANSWERS)

		TRUE	FALSE
1	A trigger, also known as a stressor, is an event or circumstance that does not result in a negative emotional response. A trigger never brings back unpleasant memories, emotions, or symptoms.		✓
2	Negative learned behavior develops as a result of negative experiences.	✓	
3	People talk negatively about others because they are happy with themselves. They have not had past trauma or negative experiences.		✓
4	People may lack insight into their reactions and have impaired judgment after experiencing a trigger, which can lead to substance abuse.	✓	
5	Even though someone might be listening, we feel that they aren't if we don't receive the response we think is correct, in the way we think is correct.	✓	
6	We never become numb and continue to look for chaos because it is the most familiar place we know how to operate from. We always release the patterns that create more chaos.		✓
7	The reality we perceive ourselves to be in is never the truth and reality we will live in.		✓
8	Positive learned behavior develops as a result of positive experiences.	✓	
9	Many times, we feel unappreciated because we are giving too much in order to feel loved and accepted.	✓	
10	The world around us is not filled with our past traumatic experiences; it doesn't send us into a space of unsafety. We don't need skills and tools to return ourselves to a state of safety.		✓

MODULE 3 SUMMARY

1 **COURSE TAKEAWAY POINT ONE**

- 3.1. How Trauma Triggers Lead to Unhealthy Patterns. Triggers are important because as we begin to recognize what affects us in our daily lives, we are able to mitigate, or lessen, negativity, pain, addiction, and trauma.

2 **COURSE TAKEAWAY POINT TWO**

- 3.2. How Negative Dialogues Feed the Trauma Cycle. Negative dialogue affects us in damaging ways, including mental health challenges, depression, anxiety, toxic stress, insomnia, anger, addiction, despair, and toxic relationships.

3 **COURSE TAKEAWAY POINT THREE**

- 3.3. Trauma Cycles Create Automatic Trauma Responses. We continue to look for chaos because it is familiar. We are unable to shift from this pattern, and that creates more chaos. In order to break this cycle, we can reprogram the brain to release this damage and reset, creating a different storage of memories.

1 **YOUR TAKEAWAY POINT ONE**

- 3.1. How Trauma Triggers Lead to Unhealthy Patterns.

2 **YOUR TAKEAWAY POINT TWO**

- 3.2. How Negative Dialogues Feed the Trauma Cycle

3 **YOUR TAKEAWAY POINT THREE**

- 3.3. Trauma Cycles Create Automatic Trauma Responses.

**DECONSTRUCTING TRAUMA
IN PERSONAL SOCIAL DEVELOPMENT**

4. POSITIVE ACTIONS
AND RECOVERY

<u>Awareness Tool</u>
We are each playing a role in every situation.
What can you learn? What is your lesson? We
don't have to take experiences personally.

REPROGRAM TO POSITIVE ACTIONS

MODULE 4

DT Book Chapter 4. Reprogram To Positive Actions

What do our Personal Challenges Look Like? Why is this Important?
Our personal challenges will look different for all of us. There are times throughout our lives when we can become bitter and worn out by our personal experiences. When this happens joy and enthusiasm for life seem to disappear. Recognizing our personal challenges is important because as we begin to see our challenges and struggles, we can then begin to address and resolve them. We are not our challenges. These challenges and experiences do not define us. We can regard them as life information to learn and grow from.

Common personal challenges can be...
*Health Crises   *Career Pressure   *Moral Compass
*Workplace Issues   *Unfair Treatment   *Failure
*Emptiness   *No Inner Peace   *Impulse Control   *Relationships
*Friendship Issues   *Obstacles, Challenges   *Moving Past Your Story
*Family Issues   *Mental Health   *Haunting Past
*Financial Crises   *Grief, Loss   *Safety, Security

Why is Someone Else's Opinion so Important? How Do We Overcome that?
Other people's opinions are important because we are social beings who
are concerned about the thoughts and feelings of others; the viewpoints of
others hold a great deal of weight for us.

People's opinions do affect us. They can make us feel included and
important, and they can even make us feel like we have some control over
our surroundings. When we find out that someone thinks in the same way
we do, it makes us feel safe without us even realizing it. When someone
doesn't agree with us and has different ideas, we may feel threatened and
unsafe. We may feel like our belief system or morals are threatened
because they don't believe in the same way.

One of the main reasons others' opinions are so important is because we
have not been taught that an opinion is just an opinion, that we can all
have different opinions, and that they don't define us or the other person.
An opinion is just an opinion. Opinions change constantly as a direct result
of our ever-changing experiences.

Overcoming someone else's opinion is important because opinions are
formed and shaped by experiences and environment. If a person's
experience and environment have not been healthy or positive they will
continue to share a cycle of trauma, negativity, and destruction. This is
very toxic and gets passed on just like a disease. We then end up with
generational trauma that poisons us all.

How Do We Label Ourselves and Others? Why is this Important?
We label ourselves and others all the time by placing judgments and
projections on each other.

Every time someone treats us badly, we take that as evidence that they are a bad person, and not just that they are a possibly good person who just happened to do a bad thing. We label ourselves and others by constantly assigning labels that pass judgment and make assumptions.

We categorize certain people as addicts, lazy, weak, narcissistic, needy, etcetera. These labels carry with them the idea that a person's behavior reflects their true nature, even though it may be a fair reflection of how they are acting in the moment. When someone treats us poorly, we interpret that as proof that they are a bad person, not just that they might be a good person who unintentionally did something bad.

Awareness Tool: Labels are dangerous and defeatist. They can lead to addictions, anger, fear, disorders, despair, health issues, and more.

Negative labels can hurt us deeply. Labels are like poison — once you believe them, you'll live up to them. Labels create trauma-related failures and unrealistic assumptions and expectations. They can destroy positive self-image. They can and do live with us for a lifetime, or at least until we learn to resolve and release them. Once we realize we are not the label, we are then able to untangle the false identities and damaging core beliefs we have adopted over time.

It is important to stop labeling because labeling is destructive and unhealthy. Let the professionals diagnose and treat because that can produce productive, positive results. The general public hurling labels and accusations at each other is not productive or positive.

We are struggling with something; it is part of the human experience.

What we feed will grow. If we feed negativity and hate, it will grow. If we feed positivity and understanding it will grow. If we were trained to understand that negative personality characteristics are not necessarily a diagnosis and that people can change if they have the opportunity to Deconstruct Trauma, we might realize that it is not appropriate to define or label ourselves or others by current behavior. We are all learning and growing through our experiences.

We have been shaped by our prior experiences but are not doomed to stay in those experiences. We can change our perceptions and actions. This wisdom and knowledge can change our lives if we are ready and open to the possibility of healing and change.

We further explore the idea that each person's journey is their own. We are not responsible for their journey or making them see the light. We release attachment to others' actions and accept accountability and responsibility by removing ourselves if a situation is unhealthy.

If we are presenting the unhealthy behavior we can reach out for professional guidance and tools to reprogram unhealthy learned behavior patterns and release trauma. We are all here to learn and evolve.

Awareness Tool: We can find compassion for people that are suffering instead of labeling them. If you come across a person with unsafe qualities… remove yourself from the situation, send them positivity, and let them continue on their journey. When we label people it keeps us trapped in that negative energy and vibration.

Awareness Tool: When we label or are labeled, we view ourselves as separate. This affects us at a fundamental level. If we are separate there is no harmony. We feel like we don't belong.

What Thoughts, Behaviors, and Ideas do We Project Onto Others? Why is This Important?

We tend to project our thoughts, behaviors, and ideas onto others because we are familiar with our own experience; familiarity creates an illusion of safety. Many times, we assume that we know what others are saying because of our own experience. However, they may have a completely different meaning and experience.

Understanding our projections is extremely important to release negativity and heal trauma. This process takes commitment. Follow our Deconstructing Trauma guide and release chaos, pain, and negativity.

Sacred Sol Healing Institute: Guide to Deconstructing Trauma
1. Awareness of negativity and desire to change.
2. Finding a solution.
3. Taking the first action that allows change.
4. Committing to repeated action to allow reprogramming.

Awareness Tool: Once we have AWARENESS of a situation, we can then begin to look for SOLUTIONS; then we MUST CHOOSE TO TAKE ACTION if we want something to change; and finally, WE MUST COMMIT TO REPEATED ACTION to allow an old habit to be removed and a new one to replace it.

How Does Our Past Trauma Play an Integral Role in Our Present Lives?
Past trauma plays an integral role in our lives because we can become
threatened by others' actions and opinions. We may create a false reality
and sense of security based on our environmental threats.

We project our own trauma experiences, behaviors, and ideas onto others in
order to keep ourselves safe. We create false identities, false realities, and
false scenarios to keep ourselves safe. We do this without even realizing it.
We have created a phenomenon of "Trauma-Related Expectations," and this
becomes not only an immediate issue but has long-term toxic effects.

These thought distortions lead to years, lifetimes, and generations of
trauma, pain, and dysfunction. This in turn compromises our relationship with
ourselves, with others, and the world around us, creating a life full of
negativity, trauma, and chaos.

*Awareness Tool: We are moving through the world with "Trauma-Related
Expectations." We expect negative results because we have experienced
those results through past trauma. These Trauma Related Expectations will
continue to harm our lives until we reprogram them and begin to heal.*

*Awareness Tool: If we have not taken the steps to Heal, we will try to
control our present surroundings because we couldn't control something that
compromised us at an earlier time in our lives.*

How Do We Release Expectations and Attachment? Why is This Important?
This is such an intense question! It brings up so many more questions and so
much invaluable information!

We release expectations and attachment by becoming the observer; we are not taking situations personally. In this way, we learn to release expectations and attachment to behaviors and situations for others, as well as for ourselves.

When we become the observer, we are not threatened by what we see in others or in ourselves. We can begin to observe situations, just like window shopping; we are not attached to any one thing. We are browsing without expectation, ego, or judgment.

We can step outside of our reactive state and wonder..."Why did I act like that? Why did I have that strong of a reaction?" "Why did they act like that? Why did they have that strong of a reaction?"

Whatever answers come are okay, because we are not our experiences, we are not our pain, we are not our thoughts, we are not our emotions, we are not our trauma, and we are not our suffering.

We will inadvertently outgrow relationships with ourselves and others as we shift and evolve. This is part of the process — just as our five year-old pants don't still fit us (nor should they), many relationships and situations won't fit us either, as the lesson has been presented and no longer fits. At this point, we can learn from these lessons and move on to another space, or we can continue the cycle of pain that came with the lesson.

Awareness Tool: All of our experiences are designed to learn from; they are not meant to torture us or others.

Releasing expectations and attachment is extremely important to not only see our own expectations, thoughts, and actions, but also to release them, because our experiences will be drastically different when we are not in a reactive state.

When we can just observe and ask ourselves, "Why is this happening?" instead of saying, "This is happening to me," we are able to release the trauma responses that no longer serve us. This allows us to process our past experiences, learn from our lessons, and move on in freedom and joy instead of living a life that is full of continual chaos and pain.

Awareness Tool: It is extremely important for us to see and release others' expectations, thoughts, and actions, because if we don't we will end up living someone else experience. This also will cause us to live a life that is full of continual chaos and pain.

How do We Know we are Enough? Why is this Important?
We know we are enough because we have been created with infinite worth and value; there is no way we can't be enough. Our actions may not always reflect infinite worth and value, but our actions do not determine our value and worth.

Knowing we are enough is the most important factor in our lives. Our entire life reflects how we feel about ourselves. If we feel like we are never enough that pain will be too great to sustain over a lifetime and we will look for ways to numb that pain and to check out from that altered reality. This false belief system can lead to drugs, alcohol, and many other addictions.

WORKSHEET 1

◆ What personal challenges have affected/triggered you negatively in your daily life?

◆ What insight did you gain about labeling and trauma projections from this module?

◆ What information in this module can assist you in deconstructing past trauma in your daily life?

◆ What part of this module empowered you?

WORKSHEET 2

Awareness Tools in Reprogramming To Positive Actions

- *Awareness Tool: Assumptions, expectations, and attachments to persons, places, or things lead to self-sabotage and altered perceptions.*

- *Awareness Tool: Labels are dangerous and defeatist. They can lead to addictions, anger, fear, disorders, despair, health issues, and more.*

- *Awareness Tool: Our perception dictates our experience, and our past experiences dictate our perception. Our perception will influence our interactions with the world around us, as well as the world inside of us.*

Labeling and Trauma Projections

- How has labeling and trauma projections contributed to unhealthy patterns in your life?

- How does labeling make you feel? How does it affect your thought processes?

List how you have been labeled.

Continue on to What do our Personal Challenges Look Like?

Read these personal challenges and mark the ones you identify with.

What do our Personal Challenges Look Like?

Our personal challenges will look different for all of us. There are times throughout our lives when we can become bitter and worn out by our personal experiences. When this happens, joy and enthusiasm for life seem to disappear.

Common personal challenges can be...

*Health Crises *Career Pressure *Moral Compass

*Workplace Issues *Unfair Treatment *Failure

*Emptiness *No Inner Peace *Impulse Control *Relationships

*Friendship Issues *Obstacles, Challenges *Moving Past Your Story

*Family Issues *Mental Health *Haunting Past

*Financial Crises *Grief, Loss *Safety, Security

Others include:

Abandonment	Exaggeration	Martyrdom
Absentmindedness	Excessive Focus on	Materialism
Abuse	Others	Mediocrity
Accidents	Excessive Sleeping	Minimizing
Accusing	Excuses	Moodiness
Acting the clown	Extremism	Narrowness
Addictions	Failure	Needing to Please
Aggression	Fantasizing	Others
Ambition	Faulty Beliefs	Negativity
Analyzing	Fears	No Fun
Anger	Feeling Needy	Non-Supportive
Anxiety	Fixed Ideas	Habits
Arguing	Focusing on the Past	Numbness
Arrogance	Foolishness	Obsessions
Attachment	Forgetfulness	Opportunism
Avoidance	Frustration	Overeating
Judgmental	Futility	Over-emotional

Read these personal challenges and mark the ones you identify with.

Opinionated
Reactive
Scattered
Ungrounded
Blaming
Blind Devotion
Boredom
Bossiness
Busyness
Can't Be Alone
Carelessness
Co-Dependency
Complaining
Compromise
Compulsion
Conflict
Confusion
Control
Cowardice
Criticism
Cruelty
Cynicism
Deceitfulness
Deception
Defensiveness
Defiance
Denial
Dependency
Depression
Deviousness
Discounting

Future Thinking
Glamours
Greed
Guilt
Hate
Hopelessness
Humorlessness
Humor
Ignorance
Ignoring
Illness
Illusions
Impatience
Impractical
Impulsiveness
Inaccuracy
Indecision
Indifference
Inertia
Inflexible character
Injury
Insecurity
Insensitivity
Intellectualization
Intolerance
Isolation
jealousy
Judging
Justifying Limitations
Lack of Commitment
Lack of Confidence

Over-exercising
Over-spending
Overwhelmed
Over-working
Pain
Perfectionism
Phobias
Poor Health
Poor Self-Esteem
Possessiveness
Poverty Mentality
Prejudice
Pride
Procrastination
Rationalization
Rebellion
Repression
Resentment
Resistance
Ridicule
Rudeness
Running Away
Sadness
Sarcasm
Seeking Approval
Self-obsession
Self-Centeredness
Self-Deception
Selfishness
Self-Pity
Self-Sabotage

Read these personal challenges and mark the ones you identify with.

Dishonesty	Lack of Creativity	Shame
Disorder	Lack of Discipline	Shyness
Disoriented	Lack of Energy	Solitude
Dominance	Lack of purpose	Status
Doubt	Lack of Trust	Stress
Drama	Laughing It Off	Stubbornness
Dreaming	Laziness	Suffering
Egotism	Living in the Past	Timidity
Emotions	Loneliness	Unexpressed Emotions
Envy	Low Energy	Vacillation
Escape	Lying	Vanity
	Malnutrition	Violence
	Manipulation	Withdrawal
		Worry

Why is Recognizing Personal Challenges Important?

Recognizing our personal challenges is important because as we begin to see our challenges and struggles, we can then begin to address and resolve them. We are not our challenges. These challenges and experiences do not define us. We can regard them as life information to learn and grow from.

Awareness Tool:

We are each playing a role in every situation. What can you learn? What is your lesson? We don't have to take experiences personally. RF

Awareness Tool:

We are each responsible for learning our own lessons. It is not our job to make sure others learn their lessons. RF

WORKSHEET 3

List a few words that describe the negative consequences that have developed in each dimension of your life from labeling and trauma projections.

Example

1 Spiritual   1 Felt like I had to hide my beliefs

THE EIGHT DIMENSIONS OF WELLNESS	NEGATIVE CONSEQUENCES OF LABELING
1 EMOTIONAL	1
2 FINANCIAL	2
3 SOCIAL	3
4 SPIRITUAL	4
5 OCCUPATIONAL	5
6 PHYSICAL	6
7 INTELLECTUAL	7
8 ENVIRONMENTAL	8

Identify how to reduce labeling and trauma projections.
What can you change? What can others change?

• LABELING AND TRAUMA PROJECTIONS

WORKSHEET 4

List a few words that describe the positive consequences or rewards that can develop in each dimension of your life from feeling included, valuable, and loved.

Example

1	Spiritual	1 I am safe in my spiritually and have peace.

THE EIGHT DIMENSIONS OF WELLNESS	POSITIVE CONSEQUENCES OF NOT BEING LABELED
1 EMOTIONAL	1
2 FINANCIAL	2
3 SOCIAL	3
4 SPIRITUAL	4
5 OCCUPATIONAL	5
6 PHYSICAL	6
7 INTELLECTUAL	7
8 ENVIRONMENTAL	8

Observe the impact of positive reinforcement in your life and how you can positively reinforce yourself and others.

WORKSHEET 5

How Does Our Past Trauma Play an Integral Role in
Our Present Lives?

PAST TRAUMA PLAYS AN INTEGRAL ROLE IN OUR LIVES BECAUSE...

BENEFITS OF RELEASING TRAUMA PROJECTIONS IN YOUR TRAUMA HEALING JOURNEY:

WORKSHEET 6

We label and project past trauma on ourselves and others by constantly assigning labels that pass judgment and make assumptions. Answer the questions below.

"Labeling and Projections in Our Personal Social Development"

◆ What is labeling? How does society negatively categorize people?

◆ How has labeling contributed to your present trauma?

◆ What repeated labels do you hear that trigger and retraumatize you?

◆ How often does labeling lead you to unhealthy coping mechanisms?

◆ What are healthy ways to reduce labeling and projections in your life?

Read "What Promotes Wellness in Your Life" on the next page.

What Promotes Wellness in Your Life

Music · Food · Meditation · Relationship with Creator · Family
Best Friend · Hiking · Relaxation · Breathing Techniques · TV
Support Group · Fishing · Camping · Basketball · Sports · Food
Dirt Bike · Own Vehicle · Own Place · Traveling · Swimming
Snowsports · Video Games · Sober Friends · Working Out
Love · Meetings · Going Out · Walks · Healthy Partners · Faith
Sober Healthy Environment · Movies · Belief · Happiness · Joy
Smiles · Crying · Sharing · Caring · Jokes · Laughter · Education
N.R.A · AA Wellbriety · Teaching · Learning · Sunny Day
Animals · Kindness · Soul Friends · New Things · Festivals
Family Gatherings · Concerts · Peace · Yoga · Positivity · Kids
Unconditional Self-Love · Trust · Recovery · Nature · Hobbies
Compassion · Reliability · Candy · Dancing · Joy Rides · Jobs
Acceptance · Mindfulness · Self-Care · Gratitude · Journaling
Values · Cleanliness · Safety · Sponsors · Communication · Sleep
Independence · Spirituality · Positive Judicial Assistance · Rehab
Healing · Mental Health Therapy · Integrity · Healthy Habits
Vacations · Healthy Skills · Consistency · Priorities · Forgiveness
Giving Back · Letting Go · Structure · Accountability · Nutrition
Responsibility · No Excuses · Awareness · Reflection · Sage
Ceremony · Traditional Ways · Cooking · Sweat Lodge · Sauna

Wellness takes effort. You can change your life, one thought, one action, one day at a time. The vibration you identify with will be reflected in your life.
Begin shifting to positive thoughts and positive actions will follow!
You can do this. You are not alone!

WORKSHEET 7

After reading "What Promotes Wellness in Your Life," answer the questions below.

- Reprogram To Positive Actions

 How can reprogramming to positive actions help you in your healing journey?

What did you learn from reading What Promotes Wellness in Your Life?

How can you apply this in your daily life?

NOTES:

Continue to Module 4 Quiz on the next page.

QUIZ ✦ MODULE 4

TRUE   **FALSE**

1   Recognizing our personal challenges is not important because as we begin to see our challenges and struggles, we shouldn't address or resolve them. It's good to repeat toxic cycles.

2   There are times in our lives when we can become bitter and worn out by our personal experiences.

3   Other people's opinions are not important; we are not concerned about the thoughts and feelings of others; the viewpoints of others don't matter to us.

4   We never project our thoughts, behaviors, and ideas onto others in an effort to create safety. There is no reason to understand our projections.

5   When we find out that someone thinks the same way we do, it makes us feel safe without even realizing it.

6   Labels are dangerous and defeatist. They can lead to addictions, anger, fear, disorders, despair, health issues, and more. We label ourselves and others by placing judgments and projections on each other.

7   We never assume that we know what others are saying because of our own experience.

8   When someone doesn't agree with us and has different ideas, we may feel threatened and unsafe.

9   Knowing we are enough is not an important factor in our lives. We don't need to feel valuable.

10 When we can just observe and ask ourselves, "Why is this happening?" instead of saying, "This is happening to me," we are able to release the trauma responses that no longer serve us.

SELF CHECK-IN — SCALE 0-10

Take an inventory of where you are. There are no rights or wrongs; this is a self-reflective check-in to see where you are doing well or where you want to improve. Rate statements below from 0 to 10.

1   I would like to resolve the personal challenges in my life.

2   I frequently feel self-conscious and uncomfortable.

3   I am not affected by other people's opinions.

4   I convince people that my opinions are right.

5   I do not negatively label others often.

6   I frequently negatively label myself.

7   I would like to work on daily compassion and tolerance.

8   I am ready to work on releasing trauma projections.

9   I realize that I can deconstruct past trauma.

10   I believe that healing is important.

We all struggle, We can all heal. You are not alone.

MODULE JOURNAL

Optional Notes

You are the miracle You've been looking for.

QUIZ ✦ MODULE 4 (ANSWERS)

		TRUE	FALSE
1	Recognizing our personal challenges is not important because as we begin to see our challenges and struggles, we shouldn't address or resolve them. It's good to repeat toxic cycles.		✓
2	There are times in our lives when we can become bitter and worn out by our personal experiences.	✓	
3	Other people's opinions are not important; we are not concerned about the thoughts and feelings of others; the viewpoints of others don't matter to us.		✓
4	We never project our thoughts, behaviors, and ideas onto others in an effort to create safety. There is no reason to understand our projections.		✓
5	When we find out that someone thinks the same way we do, it makes us feel safe without even realizing it.	✓	
6	Labels are dangerous and defeatist. They can lead to addictions, anger, fear, disorders, despair, health issues, and more. We label ourselves and others by placing judgments and projections on each other.	✓	
7	We never assume that we know what others are saying because of our own experience.		✓
8	When someone doesn't agree with us and has different ideas, we may feel threatened and unsafe.	✓	
9	Knowing we are enough is not an important factor in our lives. We don't need to feel valuable.		✓
10	When we can just observe and ask ourselves, "Why is this happening?" instead of saying, "This is happening to me," we are able to release the trauma responses that no longer serve us.	✓	

MODULE 4 SUMMARY

COURSE TAKEAWAY POINT ONE

1

- 4.1. Personal Challenges in Trauma Healing. Recognizing our personal challenges is important because, as we begin to see our challenges and struggles, we can then begin to address and resolve them.

COURSE TAKEAWAY POINT TWO

2

- 4.2. Labeling and Trauma Projections. It is important to stop labeling. Labeling is destructive and unhealthy. What we feed will grow. If we feed negativity and hate, it will grow. If we feed positivity and understanding, it will grow.

COURSE TAKEAWAY POINT THREE

3

- 4.3. Deconstructing Past Trauma. We project our own trauma experiences, behaviors, and ideas onto others to keep ourselves safe. We also develop false identities, false realities, and false scenarios seeking safety. These "Trauma-Related Expectations" create immediate and long-term toxic effects.

YOUR TAKEAWAY POINT ONE

1

- 4.1. Personal Challenges in Trauma Healing.

YOUR TAKEAWAY POINT TWO

2

- 4.2. Labeling and Trauma Projections.

YOUR TAKEAWAY POINT THREE

3

- 4.3. Deconstructing Past Trauma.

DT: REPROGRAM TO POSITIVE ACTIONS

DECONSTRUCTING TRAUMA
IN PERSONAL SOCIAL DEVELOPMENT

5. HEALTHY
RELATIONSHIPS

<u>Awareness Tool</u>
Consider your relationship health. Understanding healthy and unhealthy patterns will allow you to choose what is appropriate for you.

HEALTHY RELATIONSHIPS

MODULE 5

DT Book Chapter 5. Healthy Relationships

What are Healthy Relationships with Others? Why is this Important? Healthy relationships with others require work and compromise from both parties, as well as honesty, trust, respect, and open communication. No one is at an unfair disadvantage. Partners treat each other with mutual respect and trust, allowing each to make their own choices without fear of criticism or punishment. Understanding healthy relationships with others is important because it allows us to choose if the relationships in our lives are a good fit. If they are not a good fit for us and are unhealthy, we can begin to determine what steps we need to take to begin to shift these relationships.

How to Know If You Are In a Healthy Relationship
From *VeryWellMind*.. Relationships are an important part of a healthy life. Research has consistently shown that social connections are critical for both mental and physical health. People who have healthy relationships have better health outcomes, are more likely to engage in healthy behaviors, and have a decreased risk of mortality.

People often spend a lot of time talking about how to spot a bad relationship, but not about what constitutes a healthy relationship.

Consider the following:
- Do you have trust in one another? Do you respect each other?
- Do you support each other's interests and efforts?
- Are you honest and open with each other?
- Are you able to maintain your individual identity?
- Do you talk about your feelings, hopes, fears, and dreams?
- Do you feel and express fondness and affection?
- Is there equality and fairness in your relationship?

Every person's needs are different. For example, some people have higher needs for openness and affection than others do. In a healthy relationship, each person is able to get what they need.

Why are Healthy Relationships with Others Important?
Understanding healthy relationships with others is important because it allows us to choose if the relationships in our lives are a good fit. If they are not a good fit for us and are unhealthy, we can begin to determine what steps we need to take to begin to shift these relationships. What are your beliefs, core values, wants, and needs out of a relationship? For example: Do you want someone that will be gentle and nurturing, or someone that will be spontaneous and exciting, et cetera?

Awareness Tool: We can begin to examine our essential, fundamental desires and needs in a relationship. Taking time to create and build a structure of what we are looking for will help us discern whether our relationships are a good fit, or if it is better to move on. We have a choice.

It is difficult to know when to let someone go; in order to protect ourselves, we must sometimes offer love from a distance. Understanding when to leave a relationship and recognizing that the sadness will pass can frequently alleviate greater suffering in the long run. Connections that are demanding, taxing, or imbalanced can have detrimental consequences on your health and well-being.

Common reasons for maintaining a relationship are the belief that the other person needs us or that they will ultimately change. Additionally, we may fear hurting the other person or lack confidence in our capacity to form new relationships. However, knowing when to stop a relationship and recognizing that the hurt will pass can frequently prevent greater suffering and a sense of loss in the long run. If you're in a relationship that isn't fulfilling or has become toxic for you, instead of trying to remedy the problem or criticizing, consider what you want from the relationship. Consider whether the other person respects your emotions.

Relationships flourish on openness, communication, mutual concern, and shared time. When one or more of these qualities are absent, it is possible that the connection, regardless of how passionate, is not worth maintaining. It is preferable to quit a relationship that doesn't seem right, rather than to continue it while harboring bitterness or animosity. On the other side, moving on without conflict may open the way to a more caring relationship in the future.

If we need to do the adjusting we can look at what is going on and why. Here we begin to reprogram our behavior patterns to accommodate a healthier relationship. If it doesn't grow our light, it doesn't belong in our lives.

If the other person needs to do the adjusting but they are not open to change or working through the challenges, it would be wise to either end or create distance in that particular relationship so we can move forward with peace. respect, happiness, and joy.

It is not our job to force others to see the light or make them understand something that they are not ready for. We each have our own journey and someone else's ability to see or not see our values and beliefs does not diminish them, or us, in any way. It is just a difference of opinion and experience.

What are Healthy Relationships with Ourselves? Why is this Important? Having a healthy relationship with yourself means being able to value yourself as a person and accept your strengths and weaknesses on a daily basis. That consideration includes self-care, self-respect, goodwill, and self-love.

It is important to have a healthy relationship with yourself because if you don't the rest of your relationships will not be healthy. We have to learn how to love ourselves first so we can show the world how we need to be loved. We cannot expect to be fulfilled and happy through other relationships in our lives if we have not created balance and happiness first inside of ourselves.

Your relationship with yourself is the most lasting relationship you will ever have. We are often told to surround ourselves with positive and encouraging people and we know the impact these relationships have. But the person that we spend the most time with, and whose voice we hear each and every day, is our own.

Awareness Tool: There is no other relationship in our lives that has as much impact as them relationship with ourselves... and yet our self-relationship is often the most neglected.

How we speak to ourselves and the way in which we treat ourselves is key to our wellbeing. An easy way to assess your relationship with yourself is to try to notice how you speak to yourself and care for yourself over the course of a day.

• Do the things you say to yourself sound like the kind of things you would say to a friend?
• Or, do you find yourself being harsh and critical?
• As you go through the day how do you treat yourself?
• Do you allow yourself time for the things that you need?
• Even something as simple as a glass of water when you feel thirsty.
• Pay attention to the things you deny yourself.

Would you ask a colleague to work through without lunch? Or refuse your child a drink? Of course, you wouldn't! And yet you may well be asking this of yourself each and every day. It can be hard to be real with ourselves. But by asking the question, "Would I ask this of somebody else?" you can begin to come to grips with the real picture of your relationship with yourself and start to set yourself on a better course.

And getting on a better path is, after all, what allows us to continue to invest in our relationships with others. We can't give out what we don't have. Our self-relationship is key.

How do We Consistently Choose and Use Boundaries? Why is this Important?

Consistently choosing and using boundaries takes effort, commitment, dedication, and strength. The consistency between our actions and attitudes is created by setting boundaries. Setting boundaries allows positive effects to take place in our self-esteem and mood.

Healthy boundaries help you achieve positive emotional health. Setting boundaries is a vital component of building one's identity and is essential for health and well-being. By specifying what you will and will not be responsible for, healthy boundaries assist individuals in defining their identity.

When we create consistency between our actions and attitudes we create internal safety and respect for ourselves. Boundaries allow a foundation of safety and respect for ourselves. Healthy boundaries help people define their individuality by identifying what they will and will not hold themselves responsible for.

Creating boundaries is vital to our physical, mental, emotional, and spiritual health and well-being. When we learn how we need to be loved, we can then show the world. How else will they know? The world will treat you the same way you perceive yourself. Our perception dictates our experience.

Awareness Tool: Setting limits is a way to be assertive and show that you respect yourself, which is good for your self-esteem and your emotional state. Your attitude toward yourself will be consistent with your actions; if you act in a manner that shows respect for yourself, you will begin to respect yourself, regardless of others' behavior toward you.

How do We Learn to Communicate without Judgment or Ego? Why is this Important?

Communicating without judgment or ego takes awareness, desire to change, learning trauma-sensitive dialogue and thought processes, as well as repeated action and effort. As long as we continue to diminish ourselves and those around us with ego and judgment, growth and evolvement will not be possible. It is important to shift ego and judgment out of our conversations with others as well as our internal dialogue, because if we are always judging and negative, we will prevent ourselves and others from experiencing joy and positivity. If we have no joy or positivity in our lives we are constantly living in a state of negativity, trauma, and fear.

How do We Communicate with Compassion and Kindness? Why is this Important?

One of the best ways to communicate with compassion and kindness is to know what you want. When we have a clear idea of what we want and how we need to be treated, we are able to meet others in a space of balance and quiet strength. We can speak our truth in a kind way for all involved; if they can't hear our truth it's okay. It's not our job to convince anyone of anything. Our job is to speak our truth kindly for all and then decide from there where to go. Things will shift one way or another; if their behavior remains the same then the relationship either won't be a good fit moving forward, or it could need to be re-established.

Communicating with compassion and kindness is important because when we are able to communicate our needs with an honest and kind dialogue, we create safety for ourselves. When we honor each person's right to have their own opinion and their own experience, we do not need to communicate in judgment or ego, no matter what their response is.

WORKSHEET 1

◆ Describe healthy and unhealthy relationships in your life.

◆ What insight did you obtain about healthy boundaries from this module?

◆ What information in this module can assist you in non-judgmental communication with yourself and others?

◆ What part of this module empowered you?

WORKSHEET 2

Awareness Tools in Healthy Relationships.

- *Awareness Tool: Meeting people where they are at instead of where we think they should be, or where we are, will change our relationships.*

- *Awareness Tool: What is the point of challenging interactions with others? Ultimately, our job is to learn from each situation and decide if it is beneficial for to us to continue in that relationship or if it has run its course and it is more appropriate to move forward in a different way.*

- *Awareness Tool: Consistently setting and using limits teaches us to focus less on others' reactions and more on our own self-esteem and attitude.*

Appropriate, Safe, and Healthy Relationships.

- How have unhealthy relationships contributed to your present trauma?

- How do unhealthy relationships make you feel? How does it affect your thought processes?

List unhealthy relationships (friends, family, partners, self, etc.).

Continue on to Characteristics of Healthy Relationships.

Notice what maybe helpful for you from this information.

Characteristics of Healthy Relationships

While all relationships are different, there are some key characteristics that help differentiate a healthy interpersonal connection from an unhealthy one.

Trust

Trust in your partner is a key component of any healthy relation- ship. Research suggests that your ability to trust others is influ- enced by your overall attachment style. Relationships experienced early in life help shape the expectations that you have for future relationships.

If your past relationships have been secure, stable, and trusting, you are more likely to trust future partners as well. If, however, your past relationships were unstable and undependable, you may have to work through some trust issues going forward.

Trust is also established by how partners treat one another. When you see that your partner treats you well, is dependable, and will be there when you need them, you are more likely to develop this trust.

Building trust requires mutual self-disclosure by sharing things about yourself. As time passes, opportunities to test and evaluate that trust emerge. As trust grows, the relationship becomes a great source of comfort and security. If you feel that you have to hide things from your partner, it may be because you lack this essential trust.

Openness and Honesty

You should be able to feel that you can be yourself in a healthy relation-ship. While all couples have varying levels of openness and self-disclo-sure, you should never feel like you have to hide aspects of yourself or change who you are. Being open and honest with each other not only helps you feel more connected as a couple, but also helps foster trust.

Self-disclosure refers to what you are willing to share about yourself with another person. At the beginning of a relationship, you may hold back and exercise more caution about what you are willing to reveal. Over time, as the intimacy of a relationship increases, partners begin to reveal more of their thoughts, opinions, beliefs, interests, and memories to one another.

This doesn't mean that you need to share every single thing with your partner. Each individual needs their own privacy and space. What mat-ters most is whether each partner feels comfortable sharing their hopes, fears, and feelings if they so choose. Healthy couples don't need to be together all the time or share everything.

Differences in opinion over how much honesty there should be in a relationship can sometimes cause problems, however. Fortunately, one study found that when people are unhappy with their partner's level of openness, they typically discuss the problem with their partner. This is a good example of how addressing a problem openly can help strengthen a relationship.

While your partner may have different needs than you, it is important to find ways to compromise while still maintaining your own boundaries. Boundaries are not about secrecy; they establish that each person has their own needs and expectations.

Healthy boundaries in a relationship allow you to still do the things that are important to you, such as going out with friends and maintaining privacy, while still sharing important things with your partner.

A partner who has unhealthy expectations of openness and honesty might expect to know every detail of where you are and what you're doing, restrict who you can spend time with, or demand access to your personal social media accounts.

Mutual Respect

In close, healthy relationships, people have a shared respect for one another. They don't demean or belittle one another and offer support and security. There are a number of different ways that couples can show respect for one another.

These include:
- Listening to one another
- Not procrastinating or stonewalling when your partner asks you to do something
- Being understanding and forgiving when one person makes a mistake
- Building each other up; not tearing each other down
- Making room in your life for your partner
- Taking an interest in the things your partner enjoys
- Allowing your partner to have their own individuality
- Supporting and encouraging your partner's pursuits and passions
- Showing appreciation and gratitude for one another
- Having empathy for one another

Affection

Healthy relationships are characterized by fondness and affection. Research has shown that the initial passion that marks the start of a new relationship tends to decline over time, but this does not mean that the need for affection, comfort, and tenderness lessens.

Passionate love usually happens during the beginning of a relationship and is characterized by intense longing, strong emotions, and a need to maintain physical closeness. This passionate love eventually transforms into compassionate love, which is marked by feelings of affection, trust, intimacy, and commitment. While those intense early feelings eventually return to normal levels, couples in healthy relationships are able to build progressively deeper intimacy as the relationship progresses. However, it is important to remember that physical needs are different for each individual. There is no right amount of affection or intimacy. The key to a healthy relationship is that both partners are content with the level of affection that they share with their partner. A nurturing partnership is characterized by genuine fondness and affection for one another that is expressed in a variety of ways.

Good Communication

Healthy, long-lasting relationships, whether they are friendships or romantic partnerships, require the ability to communicate well. One study found that a couple's communication style was more important than stress, commitment, and personality in predicting whether married couples would eventually divorce.

While it might seem like the best relationships are those that don't involve conflict, knowing how to argue and resolve differences of opinion effectively is more important than simply avoiding arguments in order to keep the peace.

Sometimes conflict can be an opportunity to strengthen a connection with your partner. Research has shown that conflict can be beneficial in intimate relationships when serious problems need to be addressed, allowing partners to make changes that benefit the future of the relationship. When conflicts do arise, those in healthy relationships are able to avoid personal attacks. Instead, they remain respectful and empathetic of their partner as they discuss their thoughts and feelings and work toward a resolution.

Give-and-Take

Strong relationships are marked by natural reciprocity. It isn't about keeping score or feeling that you owe the other person. You do things for one another because you genuinely want to.

This also doesn't mean that the give-and-take in a relationship is always 100% equal. At times, one partner may need more help and support. In other cases, one partner may simply prefer to take more of a caregiver role. Such imbalances are fine as long as each person is ok with the dynamic and both partners are getting the support that they need.

Awareness Tool:
Trust, openness, honesty, respect, affection, communication, and equal participation are characteristics of a healthy relationship. RF

Signs of Problems in a Relationship

Relationships can change over time and not every relationship is 100% healthy all the time. Times of stress, in particular, can lead to unhealthy behaviors and coping mechanisms that can create problems.

A relationship is unhealthy when the bad outweighs the good or when certain behaviors are harmful to one or both individuals.

- Attempts to control your behaviors
- Avoiding one another
- Being afraid to share your opinions or thoughts
- Being pressured to quit the things you enjoy
- Criticizing what you do, who you spend time with, how you dress, etc.
- Feeling pressured to change who you are
- Feeling that spending time together is an obligation
- Lack of fairness when settling conflicts
- Lack of privacy or pressure to share every detail of your life with your partner
- Neglecting your own needs to put your partner first
- Poor communication
- Unequal control over shared resources including money and transportation
- Yelling

Some problems may be temporary and something that you can address together, either through self-help methods or by consulting a mental health professional.

When it comes to more serious problems, such as abusive behaviors, your primary concern should be on maintaining your safety and security.

If you or a loved one are a victim of domestic violence, contact the National Domestic Violence Hotline at 1-800- 799-7233 for confidential assistance from trained advocates.

(For more mental health resources, you call also see VeryWellMind's National Helpline Database.

How to Build a Healthier Relationship

Toxic behaviors are often a sign that an unhealthy relationship should end. For other problems, there are many ways to fix weaknesses and build a healthier relationship.

Show Appreciation

Couples who feel gratitude for one another feel closer to one another and tend to be more satisfied with their relationships. One study published in the journal *Personal Relationships* found that showing gratitude for a partner can be an important way to boost satisfaction in romantic relationships.
Another study found that feeling gratitude for a romantic partner was a predictor of whether a relationship would last.

Keep Things Interesting

Keeping up with the daily grind of work and kids can sometimes cause couples to fall into the same old routine. Boredom can lead to greater dissatisfaction as a relationship goes on. Researchers have found, for example, that couples who reported feeling bored in the seventh year of their relationship were more likely to experience marital dissatisfaction nine years later.

Things that you can do to keep the romance alive over the long term.

- Make time for one another; schedule in dates or set aside time each week to focus on one another
- Try new things together; take a class or try a new hobby that you can both enjoy
- Break out of the same old routine
- Look for ways to surprise each other
- Spend time apart once in a while
- Turn off digital devices and spend time focused only on one another
- Find time for intimacy

Recap

Steps you can take that may help make your relationship healthier include showing appreciation for your partner and finding ways to keep the relationship interesting.

When to Seek Help

All relationships are going to have their bumps in the road. Conflicts over finances, the challenges of parenting, and other differences can all create ups and downs in a long-term relationship. Even if you and your partner have a healthy relationship most of the time, problems might sometimes arise that might benefit from professional help.

If you feel like your relationship might benefit from outside help, consider talking to a counselor or therapist. A mental health professional skilled in addressing interpersonal and relationship issues can help you both learn to communicate, listen, and cope with some of the issues that might be challenging your relationship.

It is important to remember that you cannot force someone to change their behavior unless they want to. If your partner is not interested or willing in going to counseling, go on your own and focus on your own needs and wellness. Work on building your social support system Work on building your social support system outside of the relationship and consider ending a relationship if it is ultimately unhealthy.

WORKSHEET 3

List a few words that describe the negative consequences that have developed in each dimension of your life from unhealthy relationships.

Example

| 1 | Environmental | 1 Negative, depressing, and toxic environment. |

THE EIGHT DIMENSIONS OF WELLNESS	NEGATIVE CONSEQUENCES UNHEALTHY RELATIONSHIPS
1 EMOTIONAL	1
2 FINANCIAL	2
3 SOCIAL	3
4 SPIRITUAL	4
5 OCCUPATIONAL	5
6 PHYSICAL	6
7 INTELLECTUAL	7
8 ENVIRONMENTAL	8

Identity how to reduce unhealthy relationships.
What can you change? What can others change?

• APPROPRIATE, SAFE, AND HEALTHY RELATIONSHIPS

WORKSHEET 4

List a few words that describe the positive consequences or rewards that can develop in each dimension of your life from appropriate, safe, and healthy relationships.

Example

| 1 Environmental | 1 Safe, happy, and peaceful environment. |

THE EIGHT DIMENSIONS OF WELLNESS	POSITIVE CONSEQUENCES OF HEALTHY RELATIONSHIPS.
1 EMOTIONAL	1
2 FINANCIAL	2
3 SOCIAL	3
4 SPIRITUAL	4
5 OCCUPATIONAL	5
6 PHYSICAL	6
7 INTELLECTUAL	7
8 ENVIRONMENTAL	8

Consider the impact of positive, appropriate, safe, and healthy relationships in your life and how you can develop these relationships.

• APPROPRIATE, SAFE, AND HEALTHY RELATIONSHIPS

WORKSHEET 5

How Does Judgmental Communication Affect The
Environment Around Us And Inside Of Us?

JUDGEMENTAL COMMUNICATION HAS AFFECTED MY LIFE IN THESE WAYS...

BENEFITS OF RELEASING JUDGMENTAL COMMUNICATION IN YOUR TRAUMA HEALING JOURNEY:

WORKSHEET 6

Healthy boundaries help you achieve positive emotional health. Setting boundaries is a vital component of building one's identity and is essential for health and well-being. Answer the questions below.

"Healthy Boundaries Keep Us Safe"

◆ What are healthy boundaries for others and yourself?

◆ How have unhealthy boundaries contributed to trauma in your life?

◆ What repeated unhealthy boundaries trigger and retraumatize you?

◆ How often do unhealthy boundaries lead you to unhealthy situations?

◆ What are healthy ways to practice healthy boundaries in your life?

Read "Our Basic Needs" on the next page.

If Our Basic Needs Have Not Been Met, We Will Struggle To Have A Healthy, Happy, Safe, And Fulfilled Life.

Maslow's Hierarchy Of Needs

Lack of our basic needs being met (food, shelter, transportation, clothes, clean water, education, mental and physical health, and access to quality health care) can lead to addictions, pain, trauma, and suffering. Mental, emotional, physical, and spiritual health challenges include depressive states, anxiety, toxic stress, insomnia, anger, hopelessness, despair, unhealthy relationships, suicide, and more.

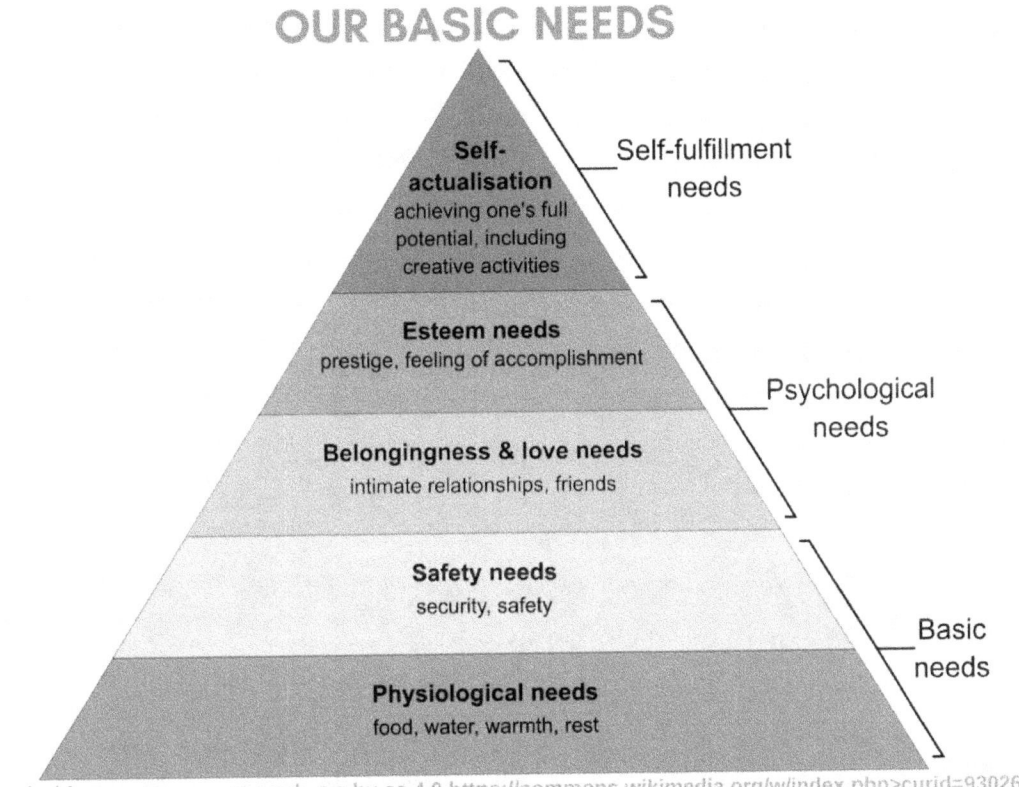

By androidmarsexpress own work, c c by-sa 4.0 https://commons.wikimedia.org/w/index.php>curid=93026655

When we begin to meet our basic needs, we can start to heal from our trauma and be successful in our life recovery. Meeting our basic needs is not a one-and-done; it is an ever-changing, fluid life experience. Our needs will continue to change as our daily environment changes.

DECONSTRUCTING TRAUMA | FOUNDATIONAL DEVELOPMENT

WORKSHEET 7

After reading "Our Basic Needs," discuss and answer the questions below.

- Healthy Relationships

 How can meeting your basic needs help you in creating healthy boundaries?

How can meeting your basic needs help you in creating healthy boundaries?

What did you learn from reading Our Basic Needs?

How can you apply this in your daily life?

NOTES:

Continue to Module 5 Quiz on the next page.

• ·HEALTHY BOUNDARIES KEEP US SAFE

QUIZ ✳ MODULE 5

TRUE   FALSE

1 Healthy relationships with others do not require work and compromise. Partners do not need to treat each other with mutual respect and trust. Unfair disadvantages help relationships.

2 Connections that are demanding, taxing, or imbalanced are good for your health and well-being.

3 Understanding healthy relationships with others is important because it allows us to choose if the relationships in our lives are a good fit.

4 Consistently choosing and using boundaries should not take effort, commitment, dedication, or strength. It should be easy. Don't try it if it's hard.

5 Understanding when to leave a relationship and recognizing that the sadness will pass can frequently alleviate greater suffering in the long run.

6 Communicating with compassion and kindness is not important. When we are able to communicate our needs with an honest and kind dialogue, we do not create safety for ourselves.

7 Setting boundaries is a vital component of building one's identity. It is essential for health and well-being.

8 When we create consistency between our actions and attitudes, we create internal safety and respect.

9 We don't need to speak our truth in a kind way. It's our job to convince everyone how to think.

10 It is important to shift ego and judgment out of our conversations with others and ourselves. If we are always judging and negative, we are not able to experience joy and positivity.

SELF CHECK-IN — SCALE 0-10

Take an inventory of where you are. There are no rights or wrongs; this is a self-reflective check-in to see where you are doing well or where you want to improve. Rate statements below from 0 to 10.

1   I would like to develop healthy relationships in my life.

2   I frequently feel confident and happy.

3   I am not affected by my relationships with others.

4   I never feel like I am right.

5   I have healthy boundaries with others.

6   I frequently have judgmental communication with others.

7   I do not have healthy boundaries with myself.

8   I want to have healthy communication with myself.

9   I realize that I can have compassion for myself.

10   I believe that I can heal.

We all struggle, We can all heal. You are not alone.

MODULE JOURNAL

Optional Notes

You are the miracle You've been looking for.

QUIZ ✦ MODULE 5 (ANSWERS)

		TRUE	FALSE
1	Healthy relationships with others do not require work and compromise. Partners do not need to treat each other with mutual respect and trust. Unfair disadvantages help relationships.		✓
2	Connections that are demanding, taxing, or imbalanced are good for your health and well-being.		✓
3	Understanding healthy relationships with others is important because it allows us to choose if the relationships in our lives are a good fit.	✓	
4	Consistently choosing and using boundaries should not take effort, commitment, dedication, or strength. It should be easy. Don't try it if it's hard.		✓
5	Understanding when to leave a relationship and recognizing that the sadness will pass can frequently alleviate greater suffering in the long run.	✓	
6	Communicating with compassion and kindness is not important. When we are able to communicate our needs with an honest and kind dialogue, we do not create safety for ourselves.		✓
7	Setting boundaries is a vital component of building one's identity. It is essential for health and well-being.	✓	
8	When we create consistency between our actions and attitudes, we create internal safety and respect.	✓	
9	We don't need to speak our truth in a kind way. It's our job to convince everyone how to think.		✓
10	It is important to shift ego and judgment out of our conversations with others and ourselves. If we are always judging and negative, we are not able to experience joy and positivity.	✓	

MODULE 5 SUMMARY

COURSE TAKEAWAY POINT ONE

- 5.1. Appropriate, Safe, and Healthy Relationships. We cannot expect to be fulfilled and happy through other relationships in our lives if we have not created balance and happiness first inside of ourselves.

COURSE TAKEAWAY POINT TWO

- 5.2. Healthy Boundaries Keep Us Safe. When we create consistency between our actions and attitudes we create internal safety and respect for ourselves. Boundaries allow a foundation of safety and respect for ourselves.

COURSE TAKEAWAY POINT THREE

- 5.3. Non-judgmental Communication. Communicating without judgment or ego takes awareness, desire to change, learning trauma-sensitive dialogue and thought processes, as well as repeated action and effort.

YOUR TAKEAWAY POINT ONE

- 5.1. Appropriate, Safe, and Healthy Relationships.

YOUR TAKEAWAY POINT TWO

- 5.2. Healthy Boundaries Keep Us Safe.

YOUR TAKEAWAY POINT THREE

5.3. Non-judgmental Communication.

**DECONSTRUCTING TRAUMA
IN PERSONAL SOCIAL DEVELOPMENT**

6. HABITS AND POSITIVE PHRASING

<u>Awareness Tool</u>
A new habit takes an average of 66 days to form and 18 to 254 days to break. We can set realistic goals and understand what is keeping us from them.

HABITS AND POSITIVE PHRASING

MODULE 6

DT Book Chapter 6. Positive Phrasing

What are Habits? Why are they Important?
A habit is a conscious, repetitive behavior. This behavior happens often because of a specific situation. As part of your morning routine, you might go brush your teeth after breakfast. A habit can be neutral, good for you, or bad for you.

Habits are important because forty percent of our actions are not conscious decisions, but habits. Habits are a big part of our lives, and a lot of the time we don't even notice them! Habits are a method used by the brain to improve performance. Because the brain programs our routines into habits, we tend to carry them out without much conscious effort. This allows us to devote our cognitive resources to more pressing matters.

How Long Does It Take to Form or Break a Habit?
It takes 18-254 days to form or break a habit. Breaking or forming habits takes awareness, desire to change, repeated action, effort, commitment, dedication, realistic goals and strength.

Negativity seems to be at the root of all unhealthy habits, so how do we break the habit of negativity? Rather than focusing on the problem, focus on the solution even if you do not know what that is yet. This will draw the solution to you rather than more blocks of the problem.

SSHI Habit-Breaking Exercise:
1. Put your hand straight out, in a stopping motion, say "NO" out loud.
2. Place your other hand flat on the center of your chest.
3. Close the eyes, inhale positivity to your body.
4. Exhale negativity out of the mouth like a sigh of relief.
5. Repeat 5-7 times.

Other options to Inhale...Exhale
Inhale: Happiness...Exhale: Sadness
Inhale: Confidence...Exhale: Doubt
Inhale: Peace...Exhale: Anger
Inhale: Courage...Exhale: Negativity
Inhale: Joy...Exhale: Grief
Inhale: Resilience...Exhale: Negativity
Inhale: Calm...Exhale: Anxiousness
Inhale: Strength...Exhale: Negativity
Inhale: Focus...Exhale: Scatter
Inhale: Freedom...Exhale: Addiction

This doesn't mean we don't allow ourselves to feel. It means that we choose what we bring in and keep; we choose what we release. We have a choice; this brings us back into empowerment. It takes practice; it takes work, just like everything else. What we feed will grow.

If we feed the negative it will grow; if we feed the positive it will grow. Give yourself permission to be happy. Give yourself permission to release negativity, permission to bring in positivity. It will change your life.

Our negative habits can be trapped by an inability to forgive. When we are not able to forgive others or ourselves fully and completely, it creates blockages of negativity that stay trapped in the mind, body, and spirit.

What is the Meaning of Forgiveness? How Can Forgiveness Change Our Lives?
The meaning of forgiveness is to overcome negative emotions. The world has a complete misperception of forgiveness. Forgiveness can change our lives because to forgive simply means to release negativity. Forgiving (releasing negativity) does not in any way condone anyone's behavior; all it does is release the negativity that keeps us trapped in the situation.

How do we Perform the Act of Forgiveness? We have to do more than just decide to forgive. We can say, "Okay, I forgive you," but it is not complete because it is only a thought. We have to follow through with actions to receive the desired result.

Coming back to releasing negativity for a moment, we know to inhale positive and exhale negative. Why is this so effective? It is so effective because that is literally the medical purpose of the breath. We inhale for the life, or breath, that we need to stay alive, and when the body exhales, it is releasing and filtering out toxins that are not good for the body.

So, when we take the natural function of something and begin to apply it in a deeper way, the results are magnified.

This is the key the world is missing. We have to use our breath to actually release the trauma, chaos, pain, and negativity from the body and mind. Otherwise, it will lay dormant and eventually reemerge, creating re-traumatization... perpetuating the cycle of trauma.

Try out the forgiveness exercise below. Stay with me, we got this! The secret to forgiveness exercise below is one of our Mindful Behavior Modification Tools. Think of a person or situation you have had trouble forgiving (can be someone else or yourself).

The Secret to Forgiveness:
1. Take 3 deep cleansing breaths to release pressure. (Inhale through nose, exhale out mouth.)
2. Gently close eyes, place palms in center of the chest and lower belly.
3. Begin to visualize the situation you would like to forgive. (Not too close if traumatic.)
4. Inhale through the nose, bring in positivity to the situation.
5. Exhale through the mouth, releasing negativity to the earth.
6. Repeat 5-10 times. Pause to feel the tension release. Feel peace.

Now, with this completely different perspective of forgiveness, we understand that by releasing the negativity of the situation with our breath, we can heal. The more negativity we release, the deeper our connection to the positive, opening endless opportunities to absorb the benefits and purpose of positive phrasing.

What is Positive Phrasing and Rephrasing? Why is this Important?
Positive Phrasing is putting together the emotional and verbal parts of a message in a way that is positive, respectful, and helpful.

Positive Phrasing is putting together the emotional and verbal parts of a message in a way that is positive, respectful, and helpful. Positive language is a way to say what is instead of what isn't.

Deconstructing Trauma means that our body language, facial expression, tone of voice, and words all reflect the same positive message. Positive phrasing and rephrasing is so important because it will change the dynamic of your relationships — not only the relationships with others but the relationship with yourself.

This style of speech and thought process is Trauma-Informed as well as Trauma-Responsive, establishing a healing-centered approach. When we begin to speak in truth and kindness while releasing attachment to our experience, we are able to offer a whole new level of compassion and understanding for all involved. We are not threatened by a difference of opinion, because we have created safety through setting deliberate and intentional boundaries.

We have taken the time to consider what is appropriate for ourselves, and are not only willing to, but insist on, creating an environment that produces safety, love and joy.

Awareness Tool: One way to stop negative behavior is by using positive affirmations.

Another effective way to produce positive thought shifts is Cognitive Behavioral Therapy. Find professional, licensed CBT therapists near you.

What is Cognitive Behavioral Therapy (CBT)? Why is this Important? Cognitive behavioral therapy focuses on changing the automatic negative thoughts that can contribute to and worsen our emotional difficulties, depression, and anxiety. Focusing on changing the automatic negative thoughts that can contribute to and worsen our emotional difficulties, depressive states, and anxiousness.

There are many ways to restructure negative mindsets into positive ones. One of the methods we work with is a Positive Behavior Resilience™ approach, which is unique to Sacred Sol Healing Institute and is part of our Deconstructing Trauma Program. Using a Positive Behavior Resilience approach consists of recognizing and replacing negative thoughts with positive thoughts, through awareness and breathwork, to facilitate deeper, lasting results.

If we continue to feed the negative mindset and habits, they will continue to have a negative effect in our lives. We have been programmed to think and perceive the world, as well as ourselves, in a negative way. This is like poison; the negativity eats away at us, and we feel like we cannot ever get ahead or do enough. So much of the information we receive is gleaned in a nonverbal way.

Our environment has a huge impact on our perception. We can learn whether we are loved or not by the simple action of someone attending or not attending to our needs. When our environment is not nurturing this creates trauma and negativity within. Perpetuating our cycle of dysfunction and chaos. We begin to live in a false reality where we are never enough. It is damaging to our mind, body, and spirit, generation after generation.

We absorb our value based on our surroundings, establishing opinions of who we are based on faulty information, filled with trauma and suffering. Recognizing that negative thoughts exist and are prevalent is key; we first have to have this awareness. Through this perspective we learn to consider options that lead to balance. Why are we upset and/or negative and how can we change that?

Positive Behavior Resilience teaches us that we can build positivity and safety inside of ourselves; we do not need others to create that space for us. We are not dependent on anyone else to create safety or happiness for us; we create this for ourselves. We are Capable, We are Loved.

Awareness Tool: We are able to break the cycle of toxic thoughts and damaging self-beliefs through awareness, positive action, and repetition.

What is MBM Dialogue? Why is this Important?
Mindful Behavior Modification (MBM) dialogue consists of conversing with others, or ourselves, without our past trauma inserting itself into our interpretations of the conversation. This dialogue is nonjudgmental, free of ego, and Trauma-Sensitive — not only for others, but also for ourselves.

Mindful Behavior Modification (MBM) dialogue is important. When we are aware of the way we think, talk and act, we realize it affects not only our lives but the lives of those around us. When we use labels in a descriptive, balanced, and non-threatening way it is not a bad thing. If we are able to use labels. in this way there is no ego, judgment, or negativity involved. We have awareness that we can utilize as a tool in a good way for discernment to understand what is healthy and what is unhealthy for our lives.

WORKSHEET 1

◆ How have your habits impacted your ability to lead a healthy, happy life?

◆ What insight did you gain about the power of positive rephrasing from this module?

◆ How can Mindful Behavior Modification assist you in your daily life?

◆ What part of this module empowered you?

Continue on to Why are Habits Important?

Notice what maybe helpful for you from this information.

Why are Habits Important?

The following article from The World Counts explains the power of habits in our lives. Habits are important because 40 percent of your actions are not conscious decisions but habits. So, habits are a big part of your life - and a lot of the time you don't even notice it!

Habits are our brain's way of increasing its efficiency. Our brain turns daily actions and behaviors into habits, so we would do them automatically and without too much thought – thus freeing up our brainpower for other more important challenges. This strategy of our brain has wonderful benefits for us. It allows us to function better in life. Just imagine if you have to consider and ponder every single task or reaction. We'd be doing nothing else but thinking! According to neuroscientist David Eagleman in Incognito: "Brains are in the business of gathering information and steering behavior appropriately."

The 3-Step Loop of Habits

To be able to change a negative habit, we have to understand how it forms. In the 1990s, a group of researchers from the Massachusetts Institute of Technology discovered a neurological process that is at the core of every habit. This simple 3-step loop is very powerful – it is hard-wired into our brain. So, to change the rules, you have to know the rules first.

1 Cue – is any trigger that tells your brain when and which habit to use.
2 Routine – is an activity, emotion or behavior.
3 Reward – is how your brain determines if a loop is beneficial to you or not.

For example: Cue – You're feeling bored. Routine - You grab a bottle of wine. Reward – You feel relaxed and happy. The cue and the reward has a very strong influence in creating habits.

It's the cause of cravings and makes you repeat behaviors or actions. But your innocent wine drinking can turn you into an alcoholic if you do it often enough. So, let's say you want to change that habit, what would you need to do?

If you only focused on changing the routine, like stop drinking wine, you will be unhappy. Your brain will think that the loop doesn't work, and it will reinforce your drinking habit. Our brain demands fulfillment and satisfaction. To be able to change a negative habit, you have to replace the routine in the loop with something else – which will also give you the same reward.

Notice what maybe helpful for you from this information.

Instead of grabbing a bottle of wine when you feel bored, try jogging or watching a good movie. These activities will offer the same reward-you will feel relaxed afterwards. Your brain will think that this particular loop works. As you do it more often, and experience the same reward, it will replace the loop where you reach for a bottle of wine when you get bored.

This 3 step loop shows you that you have the power to change a bad habit that's causing you more harm than good.

The power of habits to create positive change

Many people have habits that they want to shake off. Smoking, for example, is a hard habit to break. People try to quit, but the cravings overwhelm them, and they fall off the wagon. It's not for lack of determination that they fail. It's lack of understanding of how habits are formed.

Since you now understand how habits take hold of our life, you could start creating new loops and forming new habits that will promote positive changes. It is possible to kick whatever bad habit is holding you back.

The following steps can help manifest positive habits in your life:

1 Examine the Routine – This would be the behavior you want to change. If being an alcoholic is a problem, what makes you do it? What satisfaction do you get?

2 Analyze the Reward – Drinking gives you hangovers and breeds other problems. But obviously, you get an immediate reward when you reach for that bottle. What is the reward? Is it an escape, the immediate feeling of relaxation or the distraction? Once you know the why of the behavior, it'll be easier to find a better habit that will give you the same reward.

3 Identify the Cue –What compels your behavior? Triggers are stealthy so you might need to observe your own behavior and take notes. What were you doing before an unwanted act? What were you feeling? What reward were you after? Being aware of the habit and what's reinforcing it is a positive way forward and is the first step to change.

Review this Daily Habit Tracker. Can use for negative or positive habits.

DAILY HABIT TRACKER EXAMPLE

POSITIIVE SUPPORT	m	t	w	t	f	s	s
Positive Friends/Groups:							
Success/Wellness Plan:							
Positive Environment:							

PHYSICAL HEALTH	m	t	w	t	f	s	s
Job/Occupation:							
Daily Hygiene & Excerise:							
Healthy Eating & Water Intake:							

MENTAL HEALTH	m	t	w	t	f	s	s
Mediation:							
Support Sessions:							
Connect with Nature:							

SPIRITUAL HEALTH	m	t	w	t	f	s	s
Spiritual Connection							
Spiritual Events:							
Community Service:							

DAILY HABIT TRACKER

_____   m t w t f s s

_____   m t w t f s s

_____   m t w t f s s

_____   m t w t f s s

• IMPACTS OF HABITS IN OUR LIVES

WORKSHEET 2

Awareness Tools in Habits and Positive Phrasing

- *Awareness Tool: Through Positive Behavior Resilience we can begin to notice the distinction between healthy negative emotions such as temporary sadness and unhealthy negative emotions such as deeply depressed states of despair.*

- *Awareness Tool: Unless we have processed and reprogrammed our trauma it is still affecting our daily lives, even if we don't realize it.*

- *Awareness Tool: If we all used Trauma-Sensitive language, it would drastically reduce challenges, misunderstandings, trauma, and pain.*

Impacts of Unhealthy Habits in Our Daily Lives.

- How did you develop unhealthy habits?

- What habits do you want to change? How do they affect your thought processes?

List your unhealthy habits.

Continue on to What is Mindful Behavior Modification (MBM) Dialogue?

Read and discuss this Mindful Behavior Modification Dialogue

Another form of positive phrasing is Mindful Behavior Modification™. This modality is also unique to Sacred Sol Healing Institute.

What is Mindful Behavior Modification (MBM) Dialogue?

Mindful Behavior Modification (MBM) dialogue consists of conversing with others, or ourselves, without our past trauma inserting itself into our interpretations of the conversation. Our dialogue rephrasing suggestions are non-judgmental, free of ego, Trauma-Informed, Trauma-Responsive and Trauma-Sensitive, not only for others, but also for ourselves.

Awareness Tool:
If we all began to speak in a Trauma-Sensitive format it would drastically reduce challenges, misunderstandings, trauma, and pain in our lives. RF

Awareness Tool:
One of our most effective tools in challenging conversations is to ask the other person, "What is your goal in this conversation?" RF

Awareness Tool:
We are ALL living in fear and lacking self-worth to some degree because of trauma we have endured. Our trauma will all look different. It comes to us all in different ways, but it is part of ALL of our lives. Our trauma doesn't have to define us. It can be a tool in which to learn from. RF

Why is MBM Dialogue Important?

Mindful Behavior Modification dialogue is important because when we are aware of the way we think, talk and act we realize it affects not only our lives, but the lives of those around us.

When we are using labels in a descriptive, balanced, and non-threatening way it is not a bad thing. If we are able to use labels in this way there is no ego, judgment, or negativity involved. We have awareness that we can utilize labels as a tool in a good way for *discernment* to understand what is healthy and what is unhealthy for our lives.

Why discernment is essential...

• MINDFUL BEHAVIOR MODIFICATION

Example:	Non-MBM Approach	MBM Approach
My partner said he doesn't want to go to the parade with me.	If he cared about me he would go. Why doesn't he love me?	He doesn't have to go with me. I can support myself by going to the parade and enjoying it.
Someone asks me to do something that is inappropriate.	I'll do it because they need help, even though it's a bad idea for me.	Speaking kindly to them: "Honesty I don't feel comfortable with that."
Someone tells me they are having a terrible day.	I'm so sorry and offer to do many things to make them feel better.	"Oh man, that sounds really tough. I will keep you in my thoughts and send positive vibes!"
Someone is mad that I didn't commit to helping them move.	I'm so sorry, I had so many things to do, I couldn't add one more thing."	I would have loved to help; my schedule didn't allow it. I'm glad you got into your new place."
Someone is upset; they say I never visit them.	"I'm so sorry. I will come as soon as I can." (Know- ing I can't or won't go).	"I'm not able to add anything at this time. I look forward to seeing you soon, have a blessed day!"
Someone wants me to watch their children.	"Okay, I can watch them, even though now I can't do what I need to do."	"I am unavailable to watch the kids, I have prior obligations. Great to see you."
Someone does not pay me for the work I have done.	I guess it's okay. I hope I get paid next time." (Or screaming at them to pay me.	"It is inappropriate to not pay me for a job we agreed upon. I cannot work for you."
A friend puts me in an unsafe situation.	I guess I am stuck because they are my friend, I hope everything turns out okay.	This is not appropriate for me, it feels unsafe. (Distance myself if it doesn't change.)
Someone is talking to me in an unkind way.	Ignore it because that's how they talk and there's nothing that can be done.	I politely ask them to speak to me in a kinder tone. (Remove myself if they can't hear me.)
Someone is constantly inserting their own agenda into my life.	This person will continue to manipulate me because that's what they do.	Remove this person from my life or lessen exposure. Say, "No thank you" frequently.

Labeling Rephrasing Examples: Someone that is struggling with trauma and fear is dominant in their relationships because they are trying to find control and safety in their life. This is misdirected. Trauma-sensitive means considering that the other party may not be aware that they could be suffering from negative learned behavior and feelings of inadequacy. Ideas below that allow Trauma-Sensitive shifts to emerge.

Label:	MBM Label Rephrase	MBM Trauma-Sensitive Awareness
Narcissist	Person living in fear because of trauma. Lacking self-worth because of trauma.	Someone that is struggling with trauma and fear of not being enough is passive-aggressive and controlling in their relationships because they are trying to trick others into loving them. They don't think they can be loved without manipulating others.
Codependents	Person living in fear because of trauma. Lacking self-worth because of trauma.	Someone that is struggling with trauma and fear of not being enough is passive in their relationships because they are trying to please others to feel good about themselves.
Control Freak	Person living in fear because of trauma. Lacking self-worth because of trauma.	Someone that is struggling with trauma and fear is dominant in their relationships because they are trying to find control and safety in their life. This is misdirected.
Addict	Person living in fear because of trauma. Lacking self-worth because of trauma.	Someone that is struggling with trauma and fear is using substances to not feel their pain because it is too much to handle.
Obsessive-compulsive	Person living in fear because of trauma. Lacking self-worth because of trauma.	Someone that is struggling with trauma and fear in their life is trying to find control and safety in their life by making sure everything is in order. This will not keep them safe.
Borderline personality disorder	Person living in fear because of trauma. Lacking self-worth because of trauma.	Someone that is struggling with trauma and fear has a hard time controlling their emotions. They do not feel safe in expressing emotions but at the same time struggles to stifle them.

WORKSHEET 3

List a few words that describe the negative consequences that have developed in each dimension of your life from unhealthy habits.

Example

| 1 | Intellectual | 1 | My habits kept me from my education. |

THE EIGHT DIMENSIONS OF WELLNESS	NEGATIVE CONSEQUENCES IMPACTS OF HABITS
1 EMOTIONAL	1
2 FINANCIAL	2
3 SOCIAL	3
4 SPIRITUAL	4
5 OCCUPATIONAL	5
6 PHYSICAL	6
7 INTELLECTUAL	7
8 ENVIRONMENTAL	8

Examine negative habits. What can you change?
What tools can you use to reprogram to positive habits?

WORKSHEET 4

List a few words that describe the positive consequences or
rewards that can develop in each dimension of your life from
creating positive, healthy habits.

Example

1   Intellectually   1   I can solve my challenges using healthy tools.

THE EIGHT DIMENSIONS OF WELLNESS	POSITIVE CONSEQUENCES OF HEALHTY HABITS
EMOTIONAL	1
FINANCIAL	2
SOCIAL	3
SPIRITUAL	4
OCCUPATIONAL	5
PHYSICAL	6
INTELLECTUAL	7
ENVIRONMENTAL	8

Consider the impact of positive habits in your life and how you
can positively influence yourself and others by creating and
maintaining healthy, positive habits.

WORKSHEET 5

Habits Have an Huge Impact in Our Lives

HABITS HAVE AN IMPACT IN CONTRIBUTING TO OUR TRAUMA BECAUSE...

BENEFITS OF RELEASING NEGATIVE HABITS IN YOUR TRAUMA HEALING JOURNEY:

WORKSHEET 6

Mindful Behavior Modification is crucial. When we begin to rephrase the way we think about people, we are able to stop feeding negativity. Answer the questions below.

"Mindful Behavior Modification in Personal Social Development"

◆ What is Mindful Behavior Modification (MBM)? How can MBM help you resolve trauma?

◆ How has negative communication contributed to your trauma cycle?

◆ What repeated communication challenges can you shift to MBM?

◆ What are a few examples of MBM dialogue you can use in your professional and personal life?

◆ When would using trauma-sensitive MBM dialogue be most helpful?

Work with the "Positive Behavior Resilience Tracker" on the next page.

POSITIVE BEHAVIOR RESILIENCE TRACKER

Your Harmful Negative Thought Write Down, Say Out Loud	Your Positive Replacement Thought Write Down, Say Out Loud	Positive Reprogramming Formula Write Down Positive & Follow Below, Repeat at Least 3-5 Times

*Write Down & Say Negative Pattern
I am afraid of letting people down.
	Write Down & Say Positive Replacement:
	I am working on creating safety for myself.
		Place: One hand on heart, one hand on belly. Close eyes.
		Say Positive: *I am working on creating safety for myself.*
		
		   Do: Inhale through the nose bringing in light
		      Exhale negativity out the mouth.
		
		   Say: I am capable I am loved

*Write Down & Say Negative Pattern
I feel like I'm not good enough for anyone or anything.
	Write Down & Say Positive Replacement:
	My value and worth feels smaller than I would like it to be I am taking action to change that
		Place: One hand on heart, one hand on belly. Close eyes.
		Say Positive: *My value and worth feels smaller than I would like it to be. I am taking action to change that.*
		
		   Do: Inhale through the nose bringing in light
		      Exhale negativity out the mouth.
		
		   Say: I am capable, I am loved

*Write Down & Say Negative Pattern
I feel like I can't trust my partner because of past experience
	Write Down & Say Positive Replacement:
	My partner is taking the steps to earn my trust I trust myself to handle what comes my way. I am working on living in the present moment
		Place: One hand on heart, one hand on belly. Close eyes.
		Say Positive: *My partner is taking the steps to earn my trust. I trust myself to handle what comes my way. I am working on living in the present moment.*
		
		   Do: Inhale through the nose bringing in light
		      Exhale negativity out the mouth.
		
		   Say: I am capable, I am loved

Goal:

Goal: Change your negative thought patterns!
This will help to change the negative thought patterns! Anytime you feel like you have a Negative Thought replace it with the Positive Replacement Thought and do the Positive Reprogramming Formula.
Do this as much as it comes into your head so you can reprogram it!

Total Times
Used:

POSITIVE BEHAVIOR RESILIENCE TRACKER   YOUR SHEET   SACRED SOL HEALING INSTITUTE

Your Harmful Negative Thought Write Down, Say Out Loud	Your Positive Replacement Thought Write Down, Say Out Loud	Positive Reprogramming Formula Write Down Positive & follow Below, Repeat at Least 3-5 Times.
*Write Down & Say Negative Pattern	Write Down & Say Positive Replacement:	Place: One hand on heart, one hand on belly. Close eyes Say Positive: Do: Inhale through the nose bringing in light Exhale negativity out the mouth. Say: I am capable I am loved
*Write Down & Say Negative Pattern	Write Down & Say Positive Replacement:	Place: One hand on heart, one hand on belly. Say Positive: Do: Inhale through the nose bringing in light Exhale negativity out the mouth. Say: I am capable, I am loved
*Write Down & Say Negative Pattern	Write Down & Say Positive Replacement:	Place: One hand on heart, one hand on belly. Say Positive: Do: Inhale through the nose bringing in light Exhale negativity out the mouth. Say: I am capable, I am loved

Total Times
Used:

Goal:

Goal: Change your negative thought patterns!
This will help to change the negative thought patterns! Anytime you feel like
you have a Negative Thought replace it with the Positive Replacement
Thought and do the Positive Reprogramming Formula.
Do this as much as it comes into your head so you can reprogram it!

WORKSHEET 7

After working with the "Positive Behavior Resilience Tracker," answer the questions below.

- Positive Phrasing and Rephrasing

◆ How can reframing negative thoughts into positive thoughts help you in your Trauma Healing Journey?

◆ What did you learn from the Positive Behavior Resilience Tracker tool?

◆ How can you apply this in your daily life?

NOTES:

Continue to Module 6 Quiz on the next page.

• THE POWER OF POSITIVE REPHRASING

QUIZ ✦ MODULE 6

TRUE   FALSE

1 A habit is a conscious, repetitive behavior. This behavior happens often because of a specific situation. A habit can be neutral, good for you, or bad for you.

2 Negativity is not at the root of all unhealthy habits, so we do not need to break the habit of negativity.

3 Habits are a method used by the brain to improve performance. This allows us to devote our cognitive resources to more pressing matters.

4 Breaking or forming habits does not take awareness, desire to change, repeated action, effort, commitment, dedication, realistic goals and strength.

5 It's good not to forgive and to create blockages of negativity that stay trapped in the mind, body, and spirit. This is how we heal.

6 Our negative habits can be trapped by an inability to forgive. Forgiveness can change our lives because to forgive simply means to release negativity. We can do this with our breath.

7 Positive Behavior Resilience teaches us that we can build positivity and safety inside of ourselves.

8 Mindful Behavior Modification (MBM) dialogue is threatening and based in ego.

9 One way to stop negative behavior is by using positive affirmations.

10 Positive Phrasing is putting together the emotional and verbal parts of a message in a way that is positive, respectful, and helpful. Positive language is a way to say what is instead of what isn't.

SELF CHECK-IN — SCALE 0-10

Take an inventory of where you are. There are no rights or wrongs; this is a self-reflective check-in to see where you are doing well or where you want to improve. Rate statements below from 0 to 10.

1. I would like to create positive habits in my life.

2. I frequently feel despair and hopelessness.

3. I am able to meet all of my own needs.

4. I don't think positive phrasing or thoughts are helpful.

5. I do not have negative habits.

6. I frequently like to hurt people with my words.

7. I would like to work on daily positive rephrasing.

8. I am ready to work on forgiving myself.

9. I realize that I can forgive others.

10. I believe that my environment is important to my happiness.

We all struggle, We can all heal. You are not alone.

MODULE JOURNAL

Optional Notes

You are the miracle You've been looking for.

QUIZ ✶ MODULE 6 (ANSWERS)

		TRUE	FALSE
1	A habit is a conscious, repetitive behavior. This behavior happens often because of a specific situation. A habit can be neutral, good for you, or bad for you.	✓	
2	Negativity is not at the root of all unhealthy habits, so we do not need to break the habit of negativity.		✓
3	Habits are a method used by the brain to improve performance. This allows us to devote our cognitive resources to more pressing matters.	✓	
4	Breaking or forming habits does not take awareness, desire to change, repeated action, effort, commitment, dedication, realistic goals and strength.		✓
5	It's good not to forgive and to create blockages of negativity that stay trapped in the mind, body, and spirit. This is how we heal.		✓
6	Our negative habits can be trapped by an inability to forgive. Forgiveness can change our lives because to forgive simply means to release negativity. We can do this with our breath.	✓	
7	Positive Behavior Resilience teaches us that we can build positivity and safety inside of ourselves.	✓	
8	Mindful Behavior Modification (MBM) dialogue is threatening and based in ego.		✓
9	One way to stop negative behavior is by using positive affirmations.	✓	
10	Positive Phrasing is putting together the emotional and verbal parts of a message in a way that is positive, respectful, and helpful. Positive language is a way to say what is instead of what isn't.	✓	

MODULE 6 SUMMARY

COURSE TAKEAWAY POINT ONE

- 6.1. Impacts of Habits in Our Lives. A habit can be neutral, good for you, or bad for you. Habits are important because forty percent of our actions are not conscious decisions; they are habits. Negativity and chaos are habits.

COURSE TAKEAWAY POINT TWO

- 6.2. The Power of Positive Rephrasing. Positive Phrasing is using the emotional and verbal parts of a message in a positive, respectful, and helpful way; it is a way to say what is instead of what isn't. This is Trauma-Informed and Trauma-Responsive, establishing a healing-centered approach.

COURSE TAKEAWAY POINT THREE

- 6.3. Mindful Behavior Modification. MBM consists of conversing with others, or ourselves, without our past trauma inserting itself into our interpretations of the conversation. This dialogue is nonjudgmental, free of ego, and trauma-sensitive, not only for others but also for ourselves.

YOUR TAKEAWAY POINT ONE

- 6.1. Impacts of Habits in Our Lives.

YOUR TAKEAWAY POINT TWO

- 6.2. The Power of Positive Rephrasing.

YOUR TAKEAWAY POINT THREE

- 6.3. Mindful Behavior Modification.

7. DAILY HEALING— RESILIENCE AND BALANCE

<u>Awareness Tool</u>

If we do not create daily balance in our environment, it will negativity affect our lives. Balance requires daily effort and action on our part; if we don't participate and create balance in our daily lives, it won't happen.

DAILY HEALING-RESILIENCE AND BALANCE

MODULE 7

DT Book Chapter 7. Daily Resilience and Balance

What is Resilience? Why is it Important?
According to the American Psychological Association, Resilience is the process and outcome of successfully adapting to difficult or challenging life experiences, especially through mental, emotional, and behavioral flexibility and adjustment to external and internal demands.

A number of factors contribute to how well people adapt to adversities, predominant among them are:

1. The ways in which individuals view and engage with the world
2. The availability and quality of social resources
3. Specific coping strategies

Psychological research demonstrates that the resources and skills associated with more positive adaptation (i.e., greater resilience) can be cultivated and practiced. Dr. Amit Sood has given the simplest and best definition of resilience, saying, "It's your ability to withstand adversity and bounce back and grow despite life's downturns."

Resilience is important because resilience empowers people to accept and adapt to situations and move forward, without becoming stuck in the experience. Focusing on resilience while reprogramming negative thought patterns and damaging core beliefs guides us to become our own best resource. It is important to remember that being resilient requires a set of skills that can be developed through time.

Developing resilience requires time, effort, and assistance from those around you; you will undoubtedly encounter setbacks along the road. It depends on both internal and environmental factors, including self-esteem and communication abilities, as well as the social support and resources available to you. Even those who are resilient go through stress, emotional turmoil, and pain.

Working through emotional pain and suffering is a sign of resilience. One of the best ways to build resilience is to take care of yourself on a daily basis, by balancing the body, mind, and spirit.

How do We Balance the Body, Mind, and Spirit? Why is this Important? We can balance the body, mind, and spirit in a variety of ways!

Exercise, getting out in nature, meditating, eating and sleeping well, taking time to relax, connecting with a higher space, et cetera. The ultimate tool to release tension and activate balance immediately is our breath.

Our breath is one of the greatest tools to release stress, tension, pain, negativity, chaos, anxiousness, depressive states, fear, anger, doubt, and more.

It is extremely important to balance the body, mind, and spirit if we expect to live a fulfilling, happy life. Just like our vehicles, we must maintain, care for, and balance our lives to have the optimum experience.

What is the Energy Body, and how do we Balance it? Why is this Important?

The energy body is pathways in the body where your energy moves. The energy field controls bodily functions, including those that are biochemical, cellular, and neurological. Therefore, any illness you experience, including pain, grief, fatigue, or other problems with life, is caused by an imbalance in your energy body and is ultimately manifested in your physical form. Energy, like water, should be moving to keep it healthy; otherwise, it becomes stagnant.

"The energy body is pathways in the body where your energy moves. The energetic body is shaped by the interactive undercurrents of breath, movement, feeling, emotion and intelligence." ~ Michele Crawford. "It is said that we have 72,000 channels of moving energy through our system. Energy, like water, should be moving to keep it fresh, otherwise it becomes stagnant."

Awareness Tool: Energy is everywhere, it is part of all things, yet we have forgotten it exists within us and around us. Our energy needs to be balanced and maintained because it affects us at fundamental levels in our body, mind, and spirit.

It is widely understood that everything is composed of energy and has its own unique pattern of vibration, called frequencies.

From an energetic perspective, the human body is made up of different layers of energy, called the "biofield". The frequencies of the biofield cannot necessarily be seen by the physical eye thus they are also called subtle energies, however, these frequencies have been measured.

For example, magnetic pulses and electric fields produced by cells and tissues on the surface of the skin can now be detected with the use of technology such as electrocardiograms, electroencephalograms, magnetocardiography, and magnetoencephalography. The energy of the biofield regulates the biochemical, cellular, and neurological processes of the physical body. This means that any dis-ease you may feel such as back pain, depression, fatigue, or other life challenges are the result of a disruption in the energy body and are ultimately expressed in the physical body.

Awareness Tool: When we maintain and balance our physical, mental, and spiritual energy, we manifest positive outcomes in our experiences with ourselves and others.

You probably have a good idea of how much energy you have every day. People often say that they have a lot of energy or that they could use more. Are you aware of how effectively care for your energetic body? A balanced nervous system requires continuous maintenance. Homeostasis is the state of balance in all living things. A healthy body can easily restore equilibrium when brainwaves are engaged in difficult situations.

Sometimes a deep psychological impact demands extra support to normalize energy.

We can balance the energy bodies in many ways: meditation, energy healing, exercise, breath work, yoga, music, dancing, singing, drumming, playing instruments, art, gardening, gathering traditional medicines, traditional ceremonies, stretching, balancing chakras, and more.

Balancing the energy body is important because it ensures life energy flow throughout the body, promoting health and well-being. Mental, emotional, and physical sickness come from energy blockages. By clearing obstructions and optimizing energy flow, you optimize body, mind, and spirit function.

At Sacred Sol Healing Institute, we educate extensively in understanding the energy system, how it affects our body, mind, and spirit and our daily interactions, within ourselves and in the world around us.

One of the modalities we have created is the MHIR System. We will touch on it briefly in this module. For more detailed instructions, refer to our deconstructing trauma guidebook or our wellness store for online options at https://sacredsolhealing.com/wellness-store/.

What is Mindful Heart Intelligence Reprogramming (MHIR)? Why is it Important?
The MHIR Positive Behavior Resilience System consists of simple life management tools that allow the reprogramming of learned behavior through a heart response, rather than a mind reaction. This training teaches breath-body awareness and recognition of heart-rate variance.

MHIR stands for Mindful Heart Intelligence Reprogramming. MHIR is important because this system offers us options that allow the release of blockages, pain, and suffering from the body, mind, and spirit.

Why do We Resist Balance? Why do We Have to Create Balance Daily?
We resist balance because we are addicted to negativity and chaos. When we are stressed the hormone cortisol is released and we get an adrenaline rush. So, unknowingly, we will continue to create negativity and chaos so we can continue to get our fix.

We have to create balance daily so we can maintain positivity and a happy fulfilled life. This is up to us; it is not anyone else's responsibility to create balance in our lives. If we do not create daily balance in our environment it will negatively affect our lives. Balance requires daily effort and action on our part. If we don't participate and create balance in our daily lives, it won't happen.

Many times, we are stuck in a cycle of self-sabotage. We would love for things to change but will not take the action to make that happen. We may stay in the negativity and trauma because we are used to it. Even though it is not good for us, we know what to expect and how to operate in that space, so we stay. It can seem like more of a risk to face the unknown than to stay in a damaging situation. Choosing to do nothing can cause suffering.

We suffer when we have awareness of a negative situation yet choose not to take the necessary action to change the outcome. We have choices. The choices we have may not always be the choices we like, but we always have a choice; even by not choosing, we are choosing to do nothing. Whatever we are familiar with we will revert to easiest.

Luckily, as we have been establishing, we can reprogram our tendencies to seek out negativity and chaos, but this requires action to see a different result.

BONUS! Download our full-size, color pdf, "Deconstructing Trauma Toolkit," at https://deconstructing-trauma.com/ This is a complimentary gift for you. Our Deconstructing Trauma Toolkit combines all the tools that have been offered throughout the Deconstructing Trauma Guidebook in one convenient reference space, plus bonus material.

Creating balance daily allows us to maintain a fulfilled positive and happy life. This is up to us; it is not anyone else's responsibility to create balance in our lives. It may take a while to catch up with us, but if we are not creating balance eventually we will experience excessive amounts of stress, sadness, despair, anger, hopelessness, anxiousness, fear, and more.

Awareness Tool: In a condition of fatigue, there is no hope since there is no energy to inspire and motivate.

When we are depressed or exhausted there is not a healthy energy flow in our body. We can change this by releasing negative energy and doing activities that bring in positive energy. Examples: yoga, energy healing, traditional ceremonies, singing, dancing, drumming, art, playing instruments, hiking, running, meditation, fishing, skiing, boating, family functions, sports, relaxing, sleeping, etc.

If we do not create daily balance in our environment it will negatively affect our lives. Balance requires daily effort and action on our part. If we don't participate and create balance in our daily lives, it won't happen.

What is a Wellness Plan? Why is this Important?
What Daily Actions are We Taking to Stay Balanced? A wellness plan is an action-oriented program that provides tools, instructions, and resources to improve one's health and overall well-being. A wellness plan can greatly improve our chances of producing positive change and successful habits.

When we focus on communication skills, social skills, and self-management skills, we are able to strengthen our vulnerabilities by changing triggers and reinforcing a positive environment. We have a better chance of success when we recognize issues, establish a plan, put it into action, and then check in to evaluate where we are at (accountability).

Wellness plans encourage intentional living and guide us in making life changes that reduce stress and illness while improving and maintaining our health and happiness. Intentional living will change your life. People who are successful at making life changes release limiting beliefs, fears, and low self-esteem. They add positive beliefs, skills, and tools that allow abundance.

Wellness plans are important because life is challenging! We have to actively participate in creating and bringing positivity into our lives to manifest desired results!

Decide the areas where you would like to make improvements and the areas where no improvement is needed. Start today! Reclaim your life, find freedom and joy, and reprogram to a positive self-belief system.

Step into a happier, healthier life; recovery is possible. You are not alone.

WORKSHEET 1

◆ What resilience and emotional strength have you gained in your trauma healing journey?

◆ What are daily tools that create healing, balance, and resilience?

◆ What information in this module can assist you in your healing process and in building wellness and success plans?

◆ What part of this module empowered you?

WORKSHEET 2

Awareness Tools in Daily Healing—Resilience and Balance

- *Awareness Tool: We can create healthy energy that will result in joy, happiness, and motivation.*

- *Awareness Tool: Energy affects all things. Focused energy becomes power, which can change people, circumstances, and situations worldwide.*

- *Awareness Tool: Success requires self-control. Self-management is a skill that must be learned. It is essential to succeed.*

Building Resilience and Emotional Strength.

- How can building resilience and emotional strength assist you in your life?

- How does building resilience and emotional strength make you feel? How does it affect your thought processes?

List ways to build resilience and emotional strength.

Continue on to check out wellness plans.

Daily Wellness Plan

With this daily wellness chart, we can see a simple break down of standard work and sleep hours. If we work and sleep eight hours we then have 8 hours left in a day, to clean and feed ourselves and our families, let alone sports and grocery shopping etc.

No wonder we are stressed and feel like there is not enough time in a day! The answer to this seemly overwhelming realization is to commit to daily and weekly balance. Each day we will do our standard daily needs and weave additional needs into the mix.

If you are not working the chart would be divided differently.

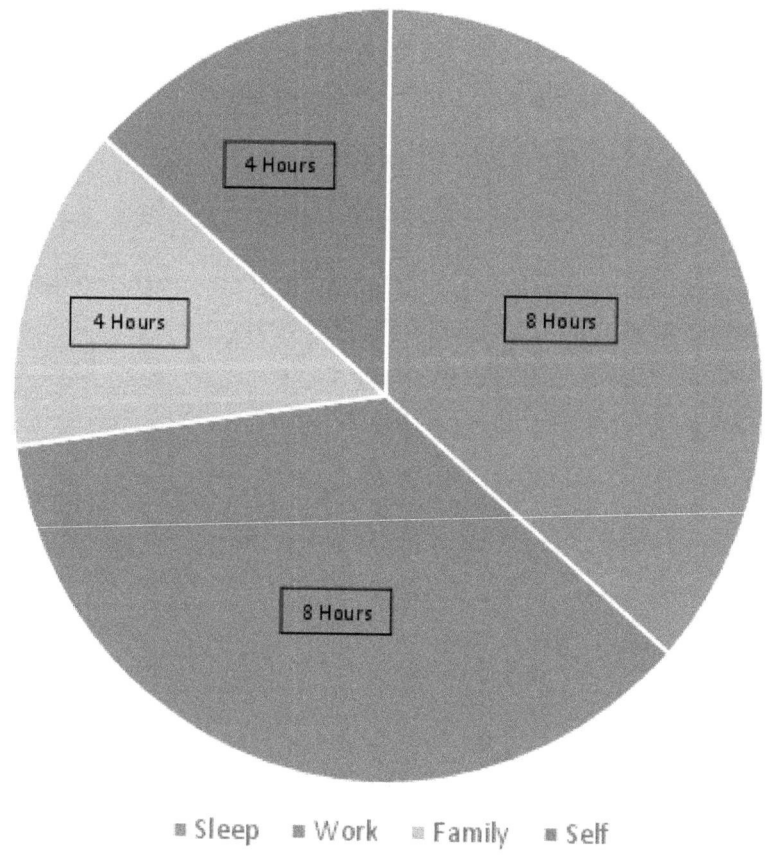

Daily Wellness Chart. 24 hours in a Day

- Sleep - Work - Family - Self

Daily Wellness Plan

My Health & Wellness Life Balance

Example of Daily Wellness Plan for a 24 hour period. We have modeled the daily wellness plan after the working person with children. Your daily wellness plan will shift according to work and family life. Customize your own plan below. Not every hour has to be used!

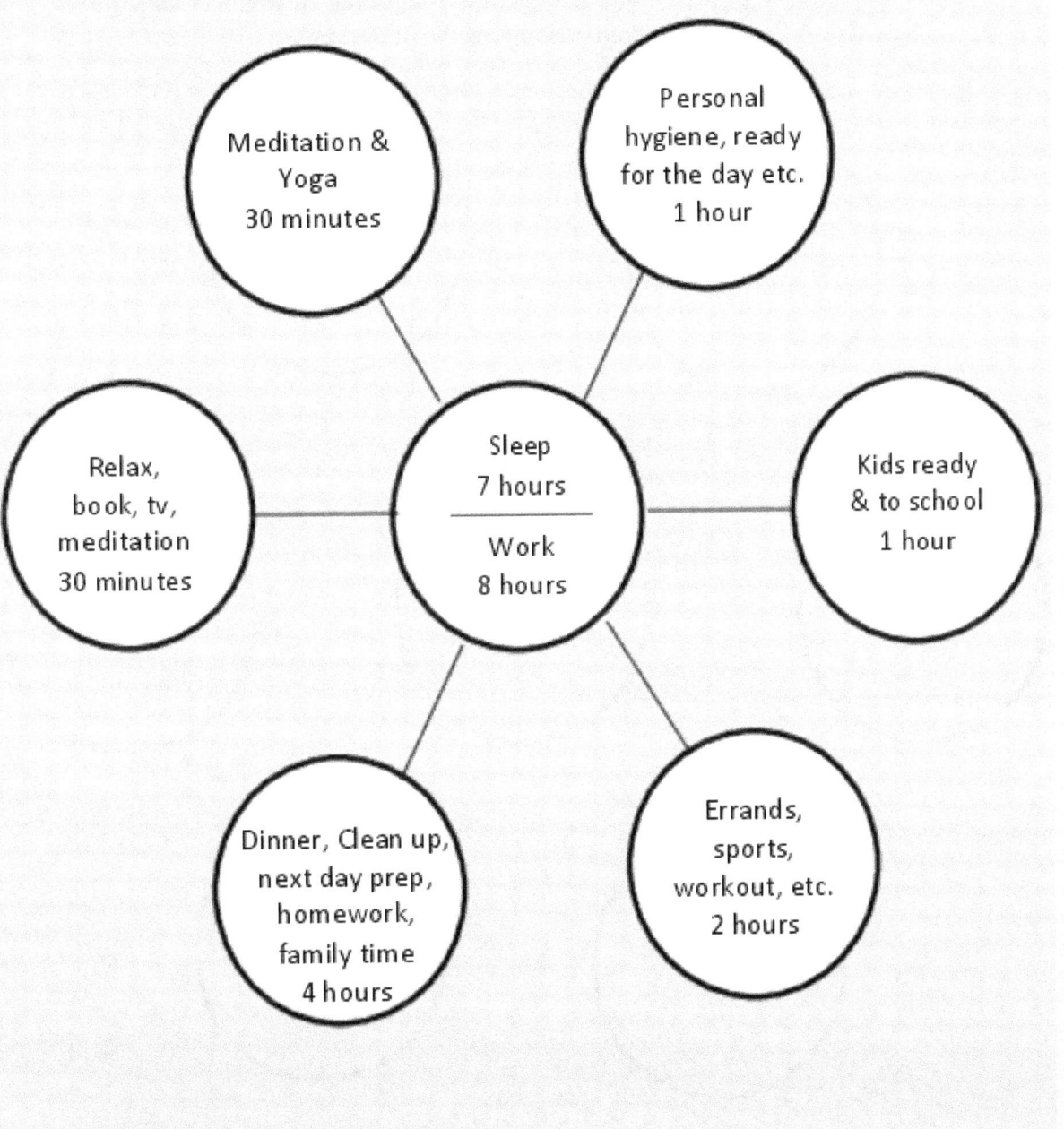

Daily Wellness Plan

My Health & Wellness Life Balance

Endless ways to use these charts! You can put yourself in the middle and use three bubbles as future goals and three as already achieved. You can put a challenge in the middle use bubbles as solutions, and or pros and cons. You can use as a hobby or recovery model, positive hobbies or actions that bring happiness to your life. Use as work/home balance three and three etc.

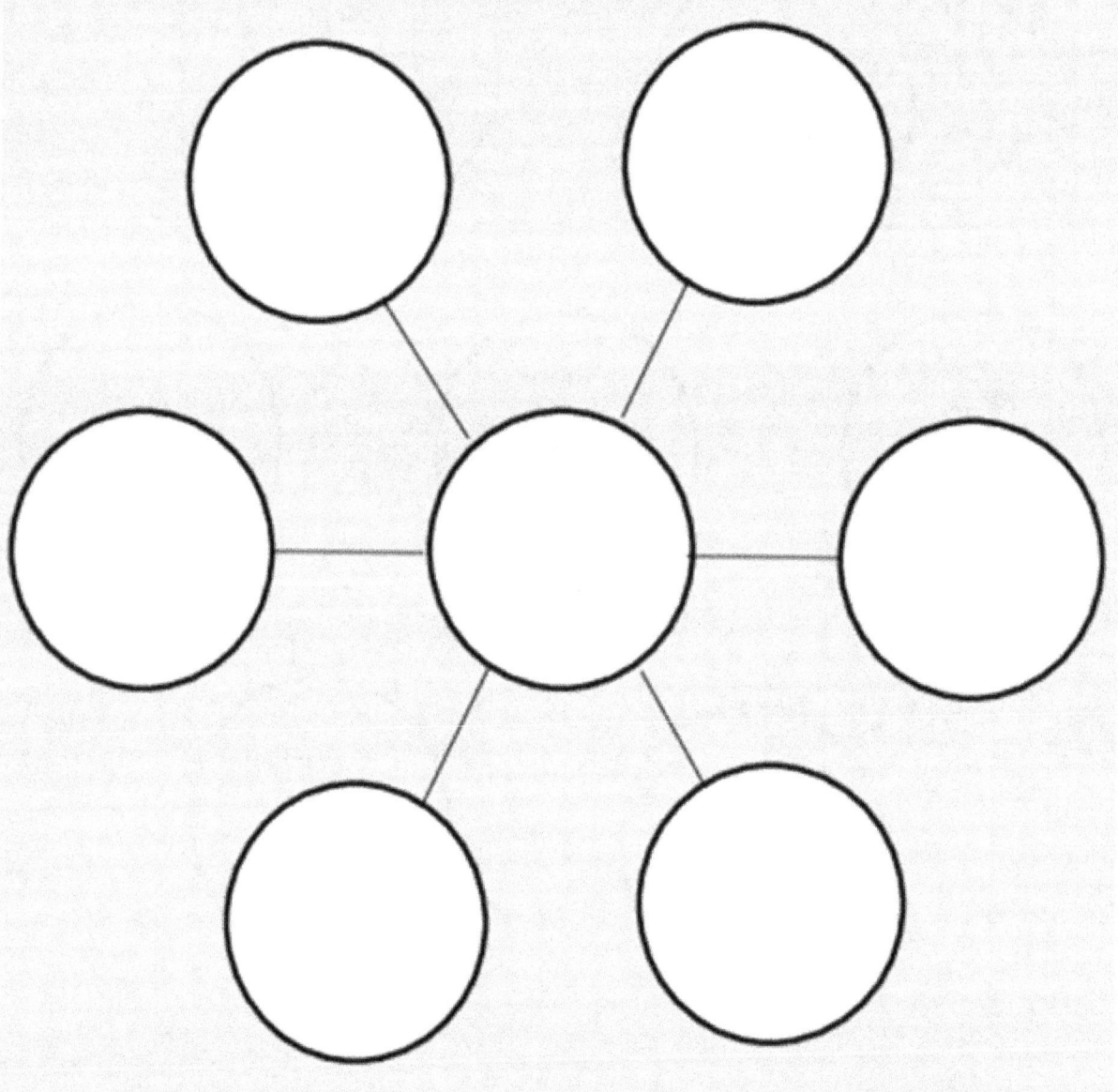

• DAILY PROGRESS AND WELLNESS PLANS

SSHI Wellness Action Plan

Wellness plans encourage intentional living and guide us in making life changes that reduce stress and illness while improving and maintaining our health and happiness. Intentional living will change your life.

People who are successful at making life changes release limiting beliefs, fears, and low self-esteem. They add positive beliefs, skills, and tools that allow abundance. Our mindful behavior modification program shifts negative thought processes and behaviors. Discover how to reprogram to positive, healthy thoughts and behavior patterns as you learn how to identify triggers and negative learned behavior.

Decide the areas you would like to make improvements and the areas that no improvement is needed. You are not alone. Start today! Reclaim your life, find freedom and joy, reprogram to a positive self-belief system. Step into a happier, healthier life.

Begin with this wellness action plan; write down, visualize, and repeat out loud your specific goals. This activates the plan of action. The moment you decide to shift your mindset from passively wanting change to actively using the tools and knowledge offered, you will see change, success, and your life will change.

List your present situation and specify your goals (what you want to accomplish). Write down, visualize, and repeat out loud your specific goals.

Keep track of your progress. Review your goals regularly. Seek assistance from others as needed. All information below is a suggestion. Consult with your medical team to create your customized plan.

Your Wellness Journey

*Wellness Action Plan for:*_____   *Start date:* _____

(Name)

Professional Health: Specific things I want to do to improve my health at my place of work
ACTION PLAN: (Reduce stress, shift work load, MBM tools, etc. ...)

Healthy Eating: Specific things I want to do to improve my eating habits.
ACTION PLAN: (Reduce chemicals and carbs, eat fruits, vegetables, fiber, protein, healthy fats...)

Weight Goal: Present weight: _____   Weight goal in 3 months:_____
ACTION PLAN: (Reduce stress, exercise regularly, healthy diet, consult personal trainer, nutritionist...)

Blood Pressure (BP): Present BP:_____   BP goal in 3 months: _____
Blood Glucose (BG): Present A1C:_____   A1C goal in 3 months: _____
ACTION PLAN: (Reduce stress, exercise regularly, healthy diet, reduce sodium, sugar...)

Blood Cholesterol: Present Total cholesterol level:_____   HDL cholesterol level: _____
Present Total cholesterol level:_____   cholesterol level: _____
ACTION PLAN: (Add foods that lower LDL, avoid trans fats, reduce saturated fats, consult nutritionist...)

Physical activity: Number of days a week I currently get 30+ min of physical activity _____
ACTION PLAN: (Walking, running, swimming, hiking, strength training, biking, yoga, dance...)

Hobbies and Interests: Develop hobbies and activities that bring positivity and joy into my life:
ACTION PLAN: (Cooking classes, art, jewelry making, scrapbook, fishing, martial arts...)

Stress and Coping: Ways I can improve mental/emotional health and coping skills:
ACTION PLAN: (Heart Breath, MBM tools, self-help, meditate, exercise, outdoors...)

Preventive Wellness: Wellness exams and services to maintain my physical and energetic health:
ACTION PLAN: (Trauma healing, energy healing, massage, chiropractor, medical exams...)

Addictive Behaviors: Habits that damage my health and family life, that I would like to change... smoking, alcohol, drugs, gambling, binge eating, anger, arguments, excessive work, excessive screen time, etc.
ACTION PLAN: (Replace harmful habits with hobbies and interests, MBM tools...)

Spiritual and Family Health: Values, virtues, or service to others I would like to incorporate into my life that would provide meaning, purpose, peace, and enrichment to my life and to others.
ACTION PLAN: (Activities with family, volunteer in community, attend nurturing services and meetings..)

Partner Health: Partner relationship Care. Daily Happiness. Positivity. Joy.
ACTION PLAN: (Date night, see a movie, board games, vacation, alone time together...)

Personal Care: Personal Care, Daily Happiness Positivity. Joy.
ACTION PLAN: (Time for yourself, take a class, pedicure, haircut, bath, massage, energy healing...)

Empowerment Questions:

Who am I? _____   Who do I want to be? _____   Where do I want to go? _____

Do I accept me? _____   3 things I like about me _____   3 things I would I like to change _____

Are any of the following behaviors familiar? Try MBM tools for any of the below.

Is this familiar: Hopeless about my circumstances never changing, others create my problems and I am powerless to change it; life is against me, stuck in life with a negative attitude, frustrated and angry, hurt when I believe loved ones don't care, resentful of people who seem happy and successful; I am exhausted, physically sick, depressed, anxious, resentful, and unfulfilled much of the time.

ACTION PLAN (explore underlying causes of symptoms, work on self-compassion, identify personal needs and goals, create a plan to achieve goals, explore reasons behind feelings of powerlessness, therapist...)

Is this familiar: I do things for people even though I don't feel appreciated; I often try to do too much, the people I spend time with make me feel bad about myself, I consistently feel dissatisfied in my job or relationships; all I do is take care of partners who do little to meet my needs; nothing I ever do is right, I am exhausted, physically sick, depressed, anxious, resentful, and unfulfilled much of the time.

ACTION PLAN: (avoid passive-aggressive behavior, express emotions, especially those of frustration and resentment, keep negative feelings from building up, set boundaries, time for personal care, therapist...)

Is this familiar: I am always trying to please people; people run over me and don't respect me; I take care of as many people as possible; I don't think very highly of myself; I get upset and take situations personally; it is a challenge to communicate my needs; if I am not taking care of people I feel lost and unaccomplished; I am exhausted, physically sick, depressed, anxious, resentful, and unfulfilled much of the time.

ACTION PLAN: (set boundaries, listen with empathy, but stop there, practice polite refusals, time for personal care, therapist. **ASK YOURSELF**: 1. Why am I doing this 2. Do I want to or have to? 3. Will this drain any of my resources? 4. Will I still have energy to meet my own needs?...)

Ultimate goal: To love yourself fully and completely. This doesn't mean we become perfect; it means we are able to face our challenges in grace and love. We learn from where we've been and choose to move forward in a different way. We release ego, judgment, guilt, shame, and fear; this is not who we are, just where we've been. We are not our trauma; we are not our pain; we are not our actions. Our actions and behaviors can shift and change as we learn. We move forward in discernment, knowing right from wrong As we shift our perception, our perspective will change. When we are able to view ourselves in a positive light, the rest of the world around us shifts to mirror that positive vibration. You are the miracle you've been looking for. It starts with you. Reprogram to a Positive Self-Belief System. You are not alone. Everything you need is already inside of you. "Heal Ourselves, Heal the World."

Commitment: INTENTIONAL LIVING WILL CHANGE MY LIFE. I CHOOSE to implement these wellness goals to the best of my ability. It is my choice to change my current situation. I do not expect others to be responsible for my happiness or my choices.

_____   _____   _____
(Signature)   (Date)   (Optional support signature)

WEEKLY PLANNER

MON

TUE

WED

THUR

FRI

SAT

SUN

WORKSHEET 3

List a few words that describe the negative consequences that have developed in each dimension of your life from not having daily resilience and balance in your life.

Example

| 1 Financial | 1 I couldn't meet basic financial needs. |

THE EIGHT DIMENSIONS OF WELLNESS	NEGATIVE CONSEQUENCES OF NOT HAVING DAILY RESILIENCE AND BALANCE
1 EMOTIONAL	1
2 FINANCIAL	2
3 SOCIAL	3
4 SPIRITUAL	4
5 OCCUPATIONAL	5
6 PHYSICAL	6
7 INTELLECTUAL	7
8 ENVIRONMENTAL	8

Consider how to create daily resilience and balance in your life. What can you change? What tools can you use?

WORKSHEET 4

List a few words that describe the positive consequences or rewards that can develop in each dimension of your life from having daily resilience and balance in your life.

Example

| 1 | Financial | 1 | I can meet my needs and have savings!! Yay!! |

THE EIGHT DIMENSIONS OF WELLNESS		POSITIVE CONSEQUENCES OF HAVING DAILY RESILIENCE AND BALANCE	
1	EMOTIONAL	1	
2	FINANCIAL	2	
3	SOCIAL	3	
4	SPIRITUAL	4	
5	OCCUPATIONAL	5	
6	PHYSICAL	6	
7	INTELLECTUAL	7	
8	ENVIRONMENTAL	8	

Observe the impact of positive daily resilience and balance in your life and how you feel when you achieve this.

Read Essential Self-Management Skills.

Awareness Tool:
We achieve daily balance in our lives by tending to all dimensions of our wellness. RF

Much of the information in our Deconstructing Trauma Program redirects our attention to the obvious and simple things we forget about in life. *Here are some quick tips from Elite Trainers.*

5 Essential Self-Management Skills

Success starts with self-management. In order to be truly productive, successful and happy, you need to develop the art of self-management. The world's greatest leaders are experts at self-management. Any position of authority or responsibility for others requires you to be able to manage yourself, before managing others. If you can master these 5 self-management skills, you'll be on track to a happy and successful life both personally and professionally.

Positivity

You can't fake true positivity. Well, not for long anyway. Positivity must come from the inside in order to be seen on the outside. The first step to developing a positive outlook is having long-term and short-term goals. Motivate yourself to achieve them with a constant stream of positivity. Refuse to allow negativity into your mind. As you complete your goals, you'll start to see a snowball effect. Keep your eyes on the end-goal and do something every day to get one step closer. Don't be too hard on yourself, and always acknowledge your successes. The thing about genuine positivity is that it's infectious. Project your positivity onto those around you and build a positive environment at work and at home.

Self-awareness

Understanding the causes of your own behavior is an incredibly important skill to have. We all know someone who is completely oblivious to their own actions, why they do them and the effect they have on others. Learn to observe yourself from an objective standpoint. Be your own manager. Ask others to judge you. At first, you may not like what you hear. However, instead of becoming defensive, make a genuine effort to remain neutral. Self-awareness is a valuable skill that few truly master. It takes years of effort to truly achieve, so start working on it today.

Stress management

Stress has ruined lives. If you're the type to make mountains out of mole-hills, you're on a fast track to an early coronary and burnout. But don't stress! There's always a solution. Implementing effective stress techniques will allow you to be proactive in managing the things that pop up in life, rather than reacting in negative ways. The energy that fuels impulsive behavior, such as angry outbursts, is the same energy that can be harnessed to motivate you to reach further and higher than ever before. When something stresses you out or drives you to anger, *use* that event as motivation. The key to managing stress effectively is delaying your initial reaction and thinking about an effective way to deal with a situation. Take the time to breathe, think and relax. Only then are you in a good state of mind to make the right choices about how to move forward.

Responsibility

Taking responsibility for your actions is step one towards true self-management. From a very young age, school teaches us to take responsibility for ourselves. However, many of us never master this skill. Prioritize your most important responsibilities. Take care of tasks as they come up, and most importantly, accept the mistakes you make. There is nothing wrong with making a mistake. There is, however, something wrong with failing to learn from a mistake. Expanding your responsibilities is exciting. Self-development is all about expanding your horizons, and that comes with responsibility. Take it, own it, and develop yourself. When you slip up (and you *will* slip up), accept it and move forward.

Productivity

The best path toward higher productivity is to manage your downtime. Got a huge load of work to knock out in a single day? Ensure you schedule breaks and enjoy them. If you've got a big year coming up, schedule a weekend where you can relax and unwind. It's impossible to operate at 100% capacity all of the time. Proper planning and time management are the key to getting the most out of your day. If you're losing focus or failing to make progress, switch tasks and come back later. Don't bang your head against a wall, it never works out.

WORKSHEET 5

Essential Self-Management Skills Can Help You Have a
Balanced, Happy, and Healthy Life.

WHAT ARE THE BENEFITS OF USING THE 5 SELF-MANAGEMENT SKILLS?

USE THE 5 SELF-MANAGEMENT SKILLS TO WORK THROUGH A CURRENT CHALLENGE.

Positivity, Self-awareness, Stress management, Responsibility,
Productivity

WORKSHEET 6

We can use daily tools to create healing, balance, and resilience in our lives. We are here in this human world to learn from our experiences. Answer the questions below.

"Daily Healing—Resilience and Balance in Our Daily Lives"

◆ How can daily tools create healing, balance, resilience, and emotional strength in your daily life?

◆ How has the lack of healthy coping skills and tools contributed to unhealthy habit and coping skills?

◆ What healthy coping skills and tools are you going to use in your trauma healing journey?

◆ How will you know when to use a healthy tool?

◆ How can resilience and emotional strength be a tool in your wellness plan?

Read "The Mindful Communication Exercise" on the next page.

• DAILY TOOLS CREATE HEALING, BALANCE, AND RESILIENCE

Mindful Communication Exercise

Try this mindfulness communication exercise!

This mindfulness communication exercise is helpful for raising communication awareness between two or more people. It allows one person to talk and one person to listen and learn about their partner, family member, or friend. We don't always have to be interested in specific things people in our lives are doing. But we can support them and grow together as we share our experiences.

Mindful Communication Exercise
Two people walk for an hour. No phones, no distractions.
Each person gets to experience both the talker and the listener.
30 minutes each. One person talks, and the other person listens and acknowledges.

Example: The listener may agree with one-word responses, nod their head, or make a sound so the talker knows they are heard.

This is not an open dialogue between two people; it is a space for the talker to share information. Each time the talker is interrupted, they stop walking as a signal to the listener that it is still their turn to talk.

- When this walk starts, set a timer for 30 minutes and decide who will be the talker first. Begin walking. When the timer goes off, both parties stop walking, and the talker wraps up what they are saying.
- The timer gets set again for 30 minutes, switches, and resumes walking. When the timer goes off, both parties stop walking, and the talker wraps up what they are saying.
- There might be times during the person's 30 minutes where they do not wish to speak; at that time, there would just be a comfortable silence.

We can also apply this exercise to a family of four or more by breaking down the time frames and keeping the walk to one hour. If there were four people, each person would have 15 minutes of talk or silent time.

Shorter walk: two people could be 30 minutes total, 15 minutes each. You can also do a much less obvious version of this exercise by practicing listening in conversations throughout your day. Always modify it to best reflect your needs.

Many times, when we are talking, we get excited and want to share because something someone says engages us. You can bring a pad of paper and a pen to write down anything you would like to share later, when your role is that of the listener. Mindfulness is an acquired skill.

How do we Balance the Body, Mind, and Spirit?

We can balance the body, mind, and spirit in a variety of ways! Exercise, getting out in nature, meditating, eating and sleeping well, taking time to relax, connecting with a higher space, having an appropriate support team in place, et cetera. However, our breath is by far the most effective tool available to release imbalance and create balance.

Awareness Tool:

The ultimate tool to release tension and activate balance immediately is... **our breath**. RF

Importance of Our Breath

Our breath is our greatest tool to release stress, tension, pain, negativity, chaos, anxiousness, despair, fear, anger, doubt, and more.
Just as we would reach for a toothbrush as the most efficient tool when cleaning our teeth, we reach for the breath when needing to release tension stress and pressure from the body, mind, and spirit. Our body is the indicator; much like a turn signal lets others know where we are headed, the body will let us know when it is in duress and uncomfortable. Our job is to learn to recognize these signals and utilize the tools that relieve this duress so we are not suffering needlessly.
The following article from DoYou.com shares simple and very effective ways to relieve stress and create balance.

Simple Ways to Balance Your Mind, Body, and Soul

When we think about health, diet, and exercise are typically the first things that come to mind. However, good health isn't just about the physical body. Our mind and body are interconnected and affect each other tremendously.

For example, a stressful situation causing negative thoughts can lead to physical pain or illness. It's important to maintain a healthy balance between your mind, body, and soul by nurturing your whole self, including your physical, mental, emotional, and spiritual needs. There are many things you can do in your daily life to achieve overall wellness.

25 simple ways to begin cultivating a mind-body-soul balance.

1. Read and learn often. Your education shouldn't stop once you're out of school. Open your mind to new possibilities, beliefs, and interests by reading, taking online classes, watching documentaries, and attending workshops.

2. Meditate regularly. Meditation improves memory, attention, mood, immune system function, sleep, and creativity. All it takes is a few minutes a day to start reaping the benefits and you can begin with this free 30-Day Meditation Challenge. Guided mediation is perfect for beginners.

3. Practice yoga. Yoga is amazing for your overall health. It helps you build strength, coordination, and flexibility while calming your mind. It also encompasses the mind-body-soul connection.

4. Avoid sitting for extended periods of time. Try to stand or move around while you work, if possible. Too much sitting is linked to heart disease, diabetes, and a shortened lifespan.

5. Get at least 15 minutes of moderate to fast-paced exercise each day. Live close to work? Walk or ride your bike on nice days. Exercise is important for heart health, physical stamina, and mood.

6. Spend time outside. Now is the perfect time of year for hiking, boating, picnics, outdoor sports, foraging for wild foods, camping, and much more!

7. Add more plant-based foods to your diet. Eating lots of vegetables and fruit can help prevent chronic disease. Shop your local farmer's market for fresh, in-season produce.

8. Get involved in a volunteer organization or activism group. Use your voice or your talents to do some good in the world. We're all connected, and it's incredible to experience that connectedness when we work toward a common goal.

9. Fuel your passions. Set aside some time each day to do what makes your soul happy. Many of us work so much that we forget how great it feels to paint, dance, make music, write, garden, or swim.

10. Listen to music often. And sing along or dance!

11. Be grateful. Take some time each day to write or think about the things you're grateful for, like family, friends, pets, food, shelter, health, or the beauty of nature.

12. Be kind to everyone. This includes yourself!

13. Get enough sleep each night. And remember that you're never too old for naps.

14. Detoxify your beauty routine. Switch to natural products.

15. Get harsh chemical cleaners out of your house. Shop green cleaners or make your own.

16. Find a career path that is meaningful to you. Chase your dreams, not riches.

17. Let go of the little things. If something won't matter tomorrow, don't let it ruin today.

18. Slow down. A little rest and relaxation when you're used to spending lots of time on the go can replenish your mind and body.

19. Stop people pleasing. There's a difference between being kind and being a doormat. If you spend too much time worrying about what others will think, you'll lose yourself and end up feeling miserable.

20. Cut major sources of stress out of your life. This includes unnecessary spending, clutter, a job you hate, or unhealthy relationships.

21. Avoid gossip and drama. Judging your neighbors and co-workers doesn't make you superior; it just makes you hard to trust.

22. Laugh often. If you take life to seriously, you're going to miss out on a whole lot of good times.

23. Travel and learn about other cultures. Do this as much as you can!

24. Forgive yourself for your past mistakes. Learn from the past, but don't let it destroy you.

25. Opt for natural remedies. With the guidance of a holistic health practitioner, herbs, the right foods, and essential oils are very healing and have fewer dangerous side effects than most pharmaceuticals.

WORKSHEET 7

After reading "How do we Balance the Body, Mind, and Spirit," answer the questions below.

- Building Resilience & Emotional Strength

◆ How can balancing the body, mind, and spirit help you in building resilience and emotional strength in your daily life?

◆ What did you learn from reading How do we Balance the Body, Mind, and Spirit?

◆ How can you apply this in your daily life?

NOTES:

Continue to Module 7 Quiz on the next page.

• BUILDING RESILIENCE AND EMOTIONAL STRENGTH

QUIZ ✦ MODULE 7

TRUE   FALSE

1   Resilience is important because resilience empowers people to accept and adapt to situations and move forward, reprogramming negative thought patterns and damaging core beliefs.

2   If we do not create daily balance in our environment, we will have a positive effect on our lives.

3   Developing resilience requires time, effort, and assistance from those around you; you will undoubtedly encounter setbacks along the road.

4   Our breath is one of the greatest tools to release stress, tension, pain, negativity, chaos, anxiousness, depressive states, fear, anger, doubt, and more.

5   The energy field does not control bodily functions, including those that are biochemical, cellular, and neurological.

6   Working through emotional pain and suffering is a sign of resilience. One of the best ways to build resilience is to take care of yourself on a daily basis, by balancing the body, mind, and spirit.

7   We resist balance because we are addicted to negativity and chaos, a cycle of self-sabotage.

8   The MHIR system increases blockages, pain, and suffering in the body, mind, and spirit.

9   When we are depressed or exhausted there is not a healthy energy flow in our body.

10 Wellness plans encourage intentional living and guide us in making life changes that reduce stress and illness while improving and maintaining our health and happiness.

SELF CHECK-IN — SCALE 0-10

Take an inventory of where you are. There are no rights or wrongs; this is a self-reflective check-in to see where you are doing well or where you want to improve. Rate statements below from 0 to 10.

1   I would like to commit to continued positivity in my life.

2   I frequently feel like I have no purpose or reason to go on.

3   I am not affected by my substance abuse.

4   I like to ignore people and be in charge.

5   I do not want to continue toxic substance abuse cycles.

6   I frequently wish I could have a happy healthy life.

7   I would like to work on a Trauma-Responsive life approach.

8   I am ready to heal and learn to love myself.

9   I realize that I am important and valuable.

10   I believe that I am capable and loved.

We all struggle, We can all heal. You are not alone.

MODULE JOURNAL

Optional Notes

You are the miracle You've been looking for.

QUIZ ✳ MODULE 7 (ANSWERS)

		TRUE	FALSE
1	Resilience is important because resilience empowers people to accept and adapt to situations and move forward, reprogramming negative thought patterns and damaging core beliefs.	✓	
2	If we do not create daily balance in our environment, we will have a positive effect on our lives.		✓
3	Developing resilience requires time, effort, and assistance from those around you; you will undoubtedly encounter setbacks along the road.	✓	
4	Our breath is one of the greatest tools to release stress, tension, pain, negativity, chaos, anxiousness, depressive states, fear, anger, doubt, and more.	✓	
5	The energy field does not control bodily functions, including those that are biochemical, cellular, and neurological.		✓
6	Working through emotional pain and suffering is a sign of resilience. One of the best ways to build resilience is to take care of yourself on a daily basis, by balancing the body, mind, and spirit.	✓	
7	We resist balance because we are addicted to negativity and chaos, a cycle of self-sabotage.	✓	
8	The MHIR system increases blockages, pain, and suffering in the body, mind, and spirit.		✓
9	When we are depressed or exhausted there is not a healthy energy flow in our body.	✓	
10	Wellness plans encourage intentional living and guide us in making life changes that reduce stress and illness while improving and maintaining our health and happiness.	✓	

MODULE 7 SUMMARY

COURSE TAKEAWAY POINT ONE

1

- 7.1. Building Resilience and Emotional Strength. Resilience is important because resilience empowers people to accept and adapt to situations and move forward, reprogramming negative thought patterns and damaging core beliefs.

COURSE TAKEAWAY POINT TWO

2

- 7.2. Daily Tools Create Healing Balance and Resilience. Exercise, nature, meditating, eating and sleeping well, relaxing, praying, wellness plans, meditation, healing, breath work, yoga, music, dancing, singing, drumming, instruments, art, gardening, traditional medicines, traditional ceremonies.

COURSE TAKEAWAY POINT THREE

3

- 7.3. Recovery Progress and Wellness Plans. When we focus on communication skills, social skills, and self-management skills, we are able to strengthen our vulnerabilities by changing triggers and reinforcing a positive environment. We have a better chance of success when we recognize issues, establish a plan, put it into action, and then check in to evaluate where we are at (accountability).

YOUR TAKEAWAY POINT ONE

1

- 7.1. Building Resilience and Emotional Strength.

YOUR TAKEAWAY POINT TWO

2

- 7.2. Daily Tools Create Healing Balance and Resilience.

YOUR TAKEAWAY POINT THREE

3

- 7.3. Recovery Progress and Wellness Plans.

8. CONCLUSION: DECONSTRUCTING TRAUMA

<u>Awareness Tool</u>
Everything is temporary; it's okay to be
uncomfortable and it's okay to not be okay.
The key is to let it pass and, if we seem to be
stuck in it, take action to change that!

CONCLUSION: DECONSTRUCTING TRAUMA

MODULE 8

DT Book Conclusion. The Collective Understanding

What is the Collective Understanding?
Everything we do affects something else. The collective understanding is arriving at a place of observation, and acceptance, for ourselves and others, without judgment or ego. In this way we can understand why we behave the way we do and take the action steps required to "Deconstruct Trauma, Release Chaos, Pain, and Negativity."

- Where is our focus? Are we living in a truthful, authentic way?
- Where are we putting our energy? How do we spend our time?
- What is our goal? Do we know?
- Are we busy feeding the chaos, triggers, and situations that we are supposed to learn from?
- Are we finding excuses to not honor what we know is right?
- What unconscious patterns or behaviors can we begin to see clearly?
- Do we really want change, or are we more comfortable in the dysfunction?
- How do we become aware?

These are all tough questions, but the answers that come are okay. We are not defined by our choices. We are definitely affected by our choices, but they are not who we are. We are human, occasional doubt will always be part of our lives as we enter new situations. We can utilize the awareness tools through this program to manage doubt, to grow and evolve from those lessons.

Committing to continued self-growth is how we heal. Unhealthy coping mechanisms are not the main issue in our lives; trauma is. As we deconstruct our trauma, we begin to release the need for unhealthy coping mechanisms. As we begin to understand and meet our unmet needs, we are able to release addictions, pain, trauma, and suffering.

We are extremely resistant to change and challenges because we have learned to identify ourselves within trauma. Just as the storm has to come for the rain to manifest, the storm comes into our life to bring about the change we need. If we were never uncomfortable we would never evolve. These challenges come to us to teach us what is not a good fit in our lives.

Negativity and chaos can push us to the point of extreme discomfort, but in small doses they can also serve a healthy purpose. If used in the appropriate way, as a guide or lesson, negativity and chaos can push us to the point of a positive change. Inappropriate behaviors are hard to change because they are useful; they help us in some way. Unhealthy environments make these behaviors more likely to happen.

As we begin to recognize negative patterns in our lives we are able to unwind and heal the trauma that lies underneath the negativity. The negativity is learned behavior, we are trying to protect ourselves.

When we begin to release the negativity and see what's underneath, we are able to resolve that pain and heal. We can "Deconstruct Trauma" through awareness and the reprogramming of negative habits. We know that the body releases chemicals from negativity and chaos, but the body also releases chemicals when we are happy and empowered.

We can release our addiction to negativity and chaos by learning from the lessons when they come and by keeping our focus on happiness and joy. Whatever we are familiar with we come back to easier. When we shift our familiarity to positivity, we will be able to get back to that positivity easier. This will create safety and balance throughout all situations, even the uncomfortable ones.

Awareness Tool: We don't have to act on our impulses; we can observe them, discover where they come from, and allow them to inspire us to change. When we resolve the trauma surrounding them we gain balance and peace.

By applying mindfulness and Trauma-Responsive skills to our daily lives, we are able to live in a positive way. Through this space we allow the busy mind to rest easy and step into the intelligence of the heart; in this way we release addictions, pain, trauma, and suffering.

The Deconstructing Trauma Program is comprised of the information and tools you have found here that release chaos, pain, and negativity. The DT Program allows us to change our perception — other people are not necessarily trying to harm us; it's not all about us. They are reacting the way they are because of their own blockages, their own triggers, their own issues, their own trauma.

When we begin to give ourselves permission to feel, along with the appropriate tools to process our feelings and heal our trauma, it can change our lives. We do not have to live in certain ways because someone else thinks we should. If they do not approve of us it is okay; we do not need anyone else's permission or approval.

Someone's opinion is just that: their opinion. It doesn't define us, just as our opinion doesn't define anyone else.

Along with growth and healing, we must leave time for integration, time for relaxation and connection. Integration allows the situation, feelings, and thoughts to settle; it may seem like we are doing nothing but just being is a necessary part of the process.

Awareness Tool: How many times have we pushed through something even though all the signs told us not to, and then we were surprised when we ended up with a bad result?

Allow time for integration; allow time for things to settle. Remember, it's like baking a cake that needs to cook for thirty-five minutes. If we take it out at thirteen minutes, it's not done; we will not have the desired result.

Awareness Tool: Instant gratification does not always create the desired result. Being patient with ourselves and others is one of the greatest tools of all.

Each time we react in an aggressive negative manner, we are being driven by a trauma trigger from the past. We most likely feel unsafe, so we are lashing out in fight-or-flight in an attempt to keep ourselves safe.

We are able to access a balanced brain by practicing self-awareness and self-acceptance. A Trauma-Informed approach leads us to feel safe to look at ourselves. Within each challenging situation our goal can be to learn, resolve, and move forward, so we are not repeating the same cycle over and over and over. These challenges come to us to learn.

One of the most effective ways to commit to continued recovery is to create a Trauma-Responsive life wellness approach through self-management. Success starts with self-management.

In order to be truly productive, successful and happy, we need to develop the art of self-management. If you can master these 5 self-management skills, you'll be on track to a happy and successful life both personally and professionally. Positivity, Self-awareness, Stress management, Responsibility, Productivity.

Awareness Tool: We don't have to take everything so personally. We can step back and observe. It's not always about us! What a relief!

We all live in our own version of perception. People can create faulty realities of events that occur.

For example, one person may have been completely traumatized and compromised by a shared event, while the other person created an adventure and likes to reminisce. The person that downplays the event creates a false reality so they can live with what has transpired.

We cannot control or force someone to see something they are not ready to see. It is their journey, is not appropriate for us to live it for them. However, it is also not appropriate for us to compromise ourselves through this process. If someone asked us to eat poison we would not take it, no matter who it was offering it. We are responsible for readjusting the relationships in our lives, to reflect safety and balance for ourselves.

What does this readjustment look like? it might go from the extreme of not being able to have any sort of relationship with someone to less drastic adjustments, such as spending less time together and being more of an observer in the relationship or being there to listen and support but not being directly involved in offering advice.

Awareness Tool: Someone may be giving their 150%. It may not be enough for us, and nowhere near our 150%, and that's okay. It doesn't mean they are bad, or that we are bad. It just means they have no more to give; we don't have to take it personally.

We may feel like someone is not participating correctly in the relationship they have with us. For example, "They wouldn't treat me the way they do if they really loved me," or "They are my parent, they should take care of me and be kind."

We perceive that they are not doing what they should because they can't give us what we need. While this train of thought is understandable, it is not balanced or Trauma-Informed. Most likely they cannot give us what we need because their own needs have not been met; they do not have the skills or tools to look past their own trauma to meet the needs of others.

This is frustrating but valuable information. The reason we don't receive what we need from others is not because we aren't good enough or they aren't good enough. It's because we can only give what is available. If we have not resolved our trauma, our availability to give will be diminished. Therefore, we adjust our relationships according to what is safe or unsafe for ourselves.

As we live through challenging life experiences, we are meant to learn and evolve. We do not have to suffer to surrender to the lesson. We can surrender the suffering.

We are not the suffering or the lesson. Discomfort can lead to growth. We don't have to suffer to heal. We are responsible for our own level of stress.

Our body holds infinite wisdom and knowledge. Once we begin to unwind and understand what the body needs we can heal in the most amazing ways. Once the physical body heals, it opens the path to healing for the mind and the spirit. It is phenomenal work!

We all have infinite worth and value beyond measure. No person or thing could validate us more than we are because it already is. Just as the mountain already is a mountain, it does not need to be validated. Just as elk is already the elk, they do not need someone to value their strengths and their endurance because it already is. You already are.

Awareness Tool: Each one of us has greatness inside. We can be extraordinary. The only way we can be truly happy is if we live in our own truth. You are the miracle you've been looking for.

WORKSHEET 1

◆ How can committing to continued self-growth assist your life wellness journey?

◆ What insight have you gained about healing and processing trauma?

◆ How can you live a Trauma-Responsive life wellness approach?

◆ What part of this course empowered you?

WORKSHEET 2

Awareness Tools in the Conclusion of Deconstructing Trauma.

- *Awareness Tool: Everything is temporary; it's okay to be uncomfortable and it's okay to not be okay. Let it pass and take action to change it!*

- *Awareness Tool: Our love for others does not need to compromise our safety or our relationships with ourselves. If it does we need to readjust and find balance. It is inappropriate to compromise one thing to have another thing grow.*

- *Awareness Tool: It's a conscious effort to not suffer, as we are conditioned to normalize suffering.*

Committing to continued self-growth.

- How will you commit to continued self-growth?

- How does committing to continued self-growth make you feel? How does it affect your thought processes?

List your steps to committing to continued self-growth.

Mindful Heart Intelligence Reprogramming™ (MHIR)

Sacred Sol Healing Institute educates extensively on understanding the energy system, how it affects our body, mind, and spirit, and our daily interactions within ourselves and in the world around us.

We are honored to share our MHIR Training Tools below. The MHIR Positive Behavior Resilience System is trademarked, held to nondisclosure standards, acknowledged, and agreed to by all who use this program. For a deeper look into the MHIR system, see our Deconstructing Trauma Guidebook.

The MHIR System consists of simple life management tools that allow the reprogramming of learned behavior through a heart response rather than a mind reaction. Based on heart math, this training teaches breath-body awareness and recognition of heart rate variance.

Utilizing the MHIR Action Tools will provide you with the ability to make cognitive decisions in stressful situations; it will build your resilience and capacity to recover from stress. Reducing stress, pain, anxiousness, and despair generates happier and healthier lives.

SACRED SOL HEALING INSTITUTE

MHIR™ Card Action Tool

Response vs. Reaction

1. MINDFUL: Non- judgmental awareness of situation. Only the facts!
2. HEART: Hands flat over chest. Inhale: Positivity, Exhale: Negativity, 4x.
3. INTELLIGENCE: Pause. Is it still significant? No: Go to 4, Yes: Repeat 1-3.
4. REPROGRAMMING: Say 3 times. I Am Capable, I Am Loved. Success!

 Renee Frye Owner/Founder
541.281.9330 541.205.6000 www.sacredsolhealing.com

Continue on to the MHIR Chart for further healing.

• HEALING AND PROCESSING TRAUMA

MHIR™ Chart Action Tool   MHIR™ Somatic Response Chart   Reprogram Behavior Patterns

Goal: Respond in a balanced, non-judgmental manner for all involved. Be patient with yourself. It takes time to learn **Response vs. Reaction!**

1) Where do you **feel this situation** in your **body? Place hand there.** Identify Body Location on Chart. Work **Down that Column** using steps 2-3.

2) Inhale **Color.** Exhale **Obstacle** out the mouth. **Repeat** 3-6 times. Continue until you feel the **Weight Lift. Pause** to become familiar with this feeling.

3) Inhale **Benefit,** Exhale out the mouth. **Repeat** 3-6 times. Continue until you feel **Content. Pause** to become familiar with this feeling.

4) Say **Affirmation 1-3 times.** Notice how you feel now. Your response may be quite different. Repeat as needed.

Distribute Energy	Energy Center 1	Energy Center 2	Energy Center 3	Energy Center 4	Energy Center 5	Energy Center 6	Energy Center 7
Body Location	Pelvis, Hips, Root	Lower Abdomen	Solar Plexus	Heart	Throat, Ears	Forehead, Temples	Crown, Top of Head
Color	Red	Orange	Yellow	Green	Blue	Purple	White
Obstacle/Block	Fear, Anger, Doubt	Guilt	Shame	Grief	Lies	Illusion	Attachment
Benefit/Balance	Secure, Safe, Support	Freedom	Infinite Worth, Value	Joy	Truth	Clarity	Unity
Affirmation	"I Have, I Am Safe, I Am Supported"	"I Can Feel, I Am Free to Be Me"	"I Trust My Own Power, I Am Enough"	"I Love, I Am Loved, I Forgive Myself"	"I Speak, I Listen to The Inner Sound"	"I See, I Rely on My Inner Guidance"	"I Am You, You Are Me, We Are One"
Meaning	Root Support	Sweetness	Lustrous Gem	Unstruck	Purification	Perceive/Command	Thousand-Fold
Sound/Element	LAM/Earth	VAM/Water	RAM/Fire	YAM/Air	HAM/Sound	OM/Light	Silent AUM/Thought
Endocrine Gland	Adrenals	Ovaries, Testicles	Pancreas	Thymus	Thyroid, Parathyroid	Pineal	Pituitary
Body Part	Eliminary System, Legs, Feet	Womb, Genitals, Bladder	Digestive System, Muscles	Heart, Lungs, Arms, Hands	Ears, Mouth, Neck, Throat, Shoulders	Eyes	Cerebral Cortex, Nervous System
Food	Meats, Proteins	Liquids	Starches	Leafy Vegetables	Fruits	Rich in Iodine	Fasting
Exercise/Pose	Grounding, Mountain	Hip Opener, Low Lunge	Core Work, Twists	Chest Opening, Camel	Open/Close, Cat Cow	Balancing, Tree	Meditate, Savasana
Malfunction	Weight Problems, Constipation	Frigidity, Impotence, Uterine Disorders	Digestive Disorders, Nervousness	Asthma, High Blood Pressure	Colds, Sore Throat, Hearing Problems	Headache, Eye Strain, Blind, Nightmares	Depression, Mental Illness, Confusion
Function	Survival, Grounding, Security	Intimacy, Desire, Pleasure	Personal Power, Will, Self Esteem	Universal Love, Self-Forgive, Compassion	Communicate, Inner Listening, Creativity	Perception, Intuition	Understand, Unity, Connect Source
Excessive Characteristics	Heavy, Overweight, Monotony, Greed	Overly Emotional, Sex Addiction, Obsessive	Dominate, Control, Aggressive, Scattered	Codependent, Poor Boundaries, Possessive	Excessive Talking, Inability to Listen	Headache, Nightmares, Delusion, Hallucinate	Spiritual Addiction, Confused, Dissociate
Deficient Characteristics	Fearful, Restless, Underweight, Spacy	Fridge, Impotent, Ridgid, Emotionally Numb	Weak Will & Self-Esteem, Passive	Lonely, Isolated, Critical Lack of Empathy	Fear of Speaking, Poor Rhythm, Deaf	Poor Memory, Denial, Unimaginative	Limited Beliefs, Materialism, Apathy
Crystal/Stone	Red Garnet, Onyx	Tiger's Eye, Sunstone	Citrine, Yellow Jasper	Rose Quartz, Jade	Lapis, Turquoise	Amethyst, Fluorite	Quartz, Selenite
Goal	Stability, Grounding, Physical Health, Prosperity, Trust	Fluidity, Pleasure, Allows Feelings, Healthy Sexuality	Vitality, Spontaneity, Purpose, Strong Self Image, Esteem & Will	Balance, Compassion, Self-Acceptance, Healthy Relationships	Creative, Variety, Clear Communicate, Resonance-richness	Psychic Perception, Clear Seeing, Accurate Interpretation	Wisdom, Knowledge Consciousness, Spiritual Connection

Continue on to the Healing Meditation.

• HEALING AND PROCESSING TRAUMA

Try this Healing Meditation.

Enjoy this Healing Meditation

In this mediation the challenge and gift presented to us is to move beyond the limits of our ego, that inner voice that likes to tell us we are not enough and to keep our guard up at all costs. Sometimes all it takes is a little shift in perspective and crown activation to realize and accept this universal truth, as we realize and accept that everything is interconnected and that we are part of the larger scheme of life, we begin to live with gratitude, faith and trust, rather than with fear and anxiety.

I will guide us through a deep relaxation technique, evoking a conscious deep sleep, allowing relaxation and expansion of awareness. Activating the relaxation response stabilizes the sympathetic and parasympathetic nervous systems, balancing the left and right hemispheres of the brain, resulting in cell regeneration and repair, as well as decreasing anxiety and improving overall well-being.

Gently soften the eyes as you read and take three deep cleansing breaths, inhale through the nose, exhale through the mouth, releasing tension throughout the body, relaxing the jaw, become aware of the natural flow of the breath, the rise and fall of the chest.

The body settles into a place of quiet and stillness, with every exhale allow your entire body to fully surrender to the earth, feel the weight of your body release, soften, melt, allow. The ground supports you; your skeletal frame supports you. Feel the freedom in the stillness of the body and mind.

Relax the muscles of the forehead, muscles around the eyes, between the eyes, eyelids, cheekbones, jaw, if you have trouble relaxing the jaw, run your tongue around your teeth in a circle, 3 times in both directions, it sound weird but totally works, relax the tongue.

Allow the neck to begin to relax, releasing the muscles all the way around. Moving down the back, the spine begins to soften, the ribs in back release.
Slowly softening the shoulders, the biceps, the triceps, the elbows. The forearms release, the wrists soften, any last bit of tension begins to work its way down the hands and gently slowly slips off the fingers to the earth beneath.

The collarbones begin to soften, the chest softens, the torso softens, the internal organs soften, the hips soften. Gently working down the legs, the thighs soften, the hamstrings soften, the shins soften, the calves soften, the ankles soften.

Any last thing that no longer serves begin to work its way down the feet and gently slowly begins to slip off the feet to the earth beneath.

You are whole, You are free
You always have been, You always will be
Here we peel back the layer to access that space
Everything you need is contained within
Pause for a moment..

Slowly begin to draw your attention back into the body, without changing anything, bring your awareness to your body, feel the ground supporting you, feel your skeletal frame supporting you. Bring your awareness to the flow of the breath at the nostrils, the sensation, of the breath. Shift your focus to the space around your body, you are more than your physical body---sense this space--- feel the power of your own presence.

Begin to inhale through the nose: "I am Capable, I am Loved."
Exhale gently out of the mouth: Sending that affirmation flowing through your body, mind, and spirit.

Gently inhale positive white light through the crown (top of the head) gently, exhale through the mouth sending this light through the body, to the feet. 2 more breaths. Slowly begin to bring movement back into the fingers and toes, allow this movement to spread through the rest of the body, arms, legs, begin to awaken, maybe a tall stretch overhead.

Gently inhale bringing the arms to the sky, exhale bringing the hands to the heart center. Place one palm flat over the Heart and the other at the lower belly.

The forgotten Miracle is the body's infinite capacity for change and renewal, we are able to reinvent our body, transforming it from a material object to a dynamic flowing process, every cell is made of awareness & energy.

We'll close today, with 3 deep cleansing breaths. Inhale thru the nose, exhale through the mouth, 2 more times. Inhale bringing in safety, love, and joy, exhale releasing any last thing that no longer serves. 1 more time, Inhale and Exhale.

Thank you so much for sharing this space with me today.

Discuss the benefits and challenges of this meditation.

• TRAUMA-RESPONSIVE LIFE WELLNESS APPROACH

SELF CHECK-IN — SCALE 0-10

Take an inventory of where you are. There are no rights or wrongs; this is a self-reflective check-in to see where you are doing well or where you want to improve. Rate statements below from 0 to 10.

1   I would like to commit to continued self-growth.

2   I frequently feel like I am not supported.

3   I want to heal and process my past trauma.

4   I frequently am bored and don't know what to do.

5   I am determined to create a safe, healthy lifestyle.

6   I feel capable and loved.

7   I am interested in a life wellness approach.

8   I understand that negative coping skills come from trauma.

9   I have a road map to a successful recovery.

10 I believe that I am the miracle I have been looking for.

We all struggle, We can all heal. You are not alone.

MODULE JOURNAL
Optional Notes

You are the miracle You've been looking for.

MODULE 8 SUMMARY

① COURSE TAKEAWAY POINT ONE

- 8.1. Committing to Continued Self-Growth. Committing to continued self growth is how we heal. Unhealthy coping mechanisms are not the main issue in our lives; trauma is. As we begin to understand and meet our unmet needs, we are able to release addictions, pain, trauma, and suffering.

② COURSE TAKEAWAY POINT TWO

- 8.2. Healing and Processing Trauma. When we begin to give ourselves permission to feel, along with the appropriate tools to process our feelings and heal our trauma, it can change our lives. Everything we do affects something else.

③ COURSE TAKEAWAY POINT THREE

- 8.3. Trauma-Responsive Life Wellness Approach. We can surrender the suffering. We can live happy, healthy lives, free of addiction and past trauma, through a Trauma-Responsive wellness approach. We are not our trauma; it is a challenge for us to learn from and grow.

---

① YOUR TAKEAWAY POINT ONE

- 8.1. Committing to Continued Self-Growth.

② YOUR TAKEAWAY POINT TWO

- 8.2. Healing and Processing Trauma.

③ YOUR TAKEAWAY POINT THREE

- 8.3. Trauma-Responsive Life Wellness Approach.

DT: CONCLUSION: DECONSTRUCTING TRAUMA

LIST OF RESOURCES

01. SACRED SOL HEALING INSTITUTE (SSHI)

SSHI. https://sacredsolhealing.com/
We are a peer-run organization that provides holistic mental wellness and substance abuse recovery support resources. We provide a healing-centered approach, meeting each person where they are at, offering hope, education, and life wellness support.

02. SUBSTANCE ABUSE AND MENTAL HEALTH SERVICES ADMINISTRATION (SAMHSA)

SAMHSA. https://www.samhsa.gov/find-help/national-helpline
National Helpline, 1-800-662-HELP (4357) (also known as the Treatment Referral Routing Service), or TTY: 1-800-487-4889 is a confidential, free, 24-hour-a-day, 365-day-a-year, information service, in English and Spanish, for individuals and family members facing mental and/or substance use disorders. This service provides referrals to local treatment facilities, support groups, and community-based organizations.

03. SUICIDE PREVENTION

988 Suicide & Crisis Lifeline. https://988lifeline.org/
We can all help prevent suicide. The 988 Lifeline provides 24/7, free and confidential support for people in distress, prevention and crisis resources for you or your loved ones, and best practices for professionals in the United States.
Suicide Prevention Resource Center. https://sprc.org/

04. YOUR LOCAL MEDICAL AND MENTAL HEALTH PROVIDERS

Online: Search "Medical and mental health providers near me."

CLOSING THOUGHTS:

As we live through challenging life experiences, we are meant to learn and evolve. We do not have to suffer to surrender to lessons. We can surrender the suffering.

We can live happy, healthy lives, free of addiction and past trauma, through a Trauma-Responsive wellness approach. We are not our trauma; it is a challenge for us to learn from and grow.

YOU ARE SPECIAL, YOU ARE VALUABLE, YOU ARE LOVED, YOU ARE MORE THAN ENOUGH.

YOU ARE WHOLE, YOU ARE FREE,
YOU ALWAYS HAVE BEEN, AND YOU ALWAYS WILL BE.
HERE WE PEEL BACK THE LAYERS TO ACCESS THAT
SPACE. EVERYTHING YOU NEED IS CONTAINED WITHIN.

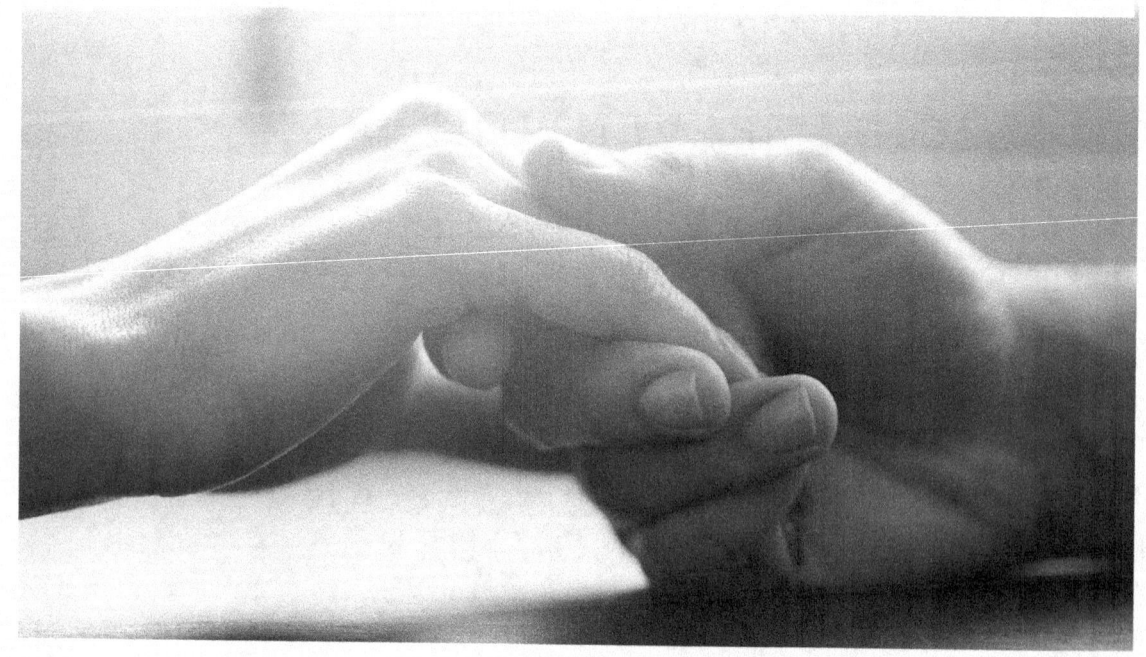

www.ingramcontent.com/pod-product-compliance
Lightning Source LLC
Chambersburg PA
CBHW080838120626
46553CB00009B/2483